THE ONE-PAGE
FINANCIAL PLAN

THE ONE-PAGE
FINANCIAL PLAN

CARL RICHARDS

A SIMPLE WAY
TO BE SMART
ABOUT YOUR
MONEY

Portfolio / Penguin

PORTFOLIO / PENGUIN
Published by the Penguin Group
Penguin Group (USA) LLC
375 Hudson Street
New York, New York 10014

USA | Canada | UK | Ireland | Australia | New Zealand | India | South Africa | China
penguin.com
A Penguin Random House Company

First published by Portfolio / Penguin, a member of Penguin Group (USA) LLC, 2015

ISBN 978-1-59184-755-7

Printed in the United States of America
1   3   5   7   9   10   8   6   4   2

Set in Bell MT Std
Designed by Alissa Rose Theodor

This publication is designed to provide accurate and authoritative information in regard to the subject matter covered. It is sold with the understanding that the publisher is not engaged in rendering legal, accounting, or other professional services. If you require legal advice or other expert assistance, you should seek the services of a competent professional.

*To the Secret Society of Real
Financial Advisors: Thank you for
the difference you're making in
the world*

CONTENTS

CONTENTS

THE ONE-PAGE
FINANCIAL PLAN

INTRODUCTION

NOT long ago I was e-mailing back and forth with Dan Heath. He's a writer—and a successful one at that. Together with his brother Chip, he has a few *New York Times* bestsellers under his belt—so he asked me what I was working on. I told him about two ideas I had been thinking about for books, and then, almost as an afterthought, I mentioned something I'd had in the back of my mind for ten years. It was a book I was thinking about writing someday called *The One-Page Financial Plan.*

"I'd buy that," he replied almost immediately.

Surprised by his response, I asked him to tell me more. I was curious since I'd only told him the title. What exactly did he think he'd be buying? Why the sudden interest?

"Creating a 'financial plan' just seems so overwhelming," he responded. "I'm going to have to meet with a lawyer and a financial planner and decide what my goals are for the rest of my life, and then face the overwhelming and depressing truth about planning for retirement (it seems you need to have $7.8 million saved by age sixty-five or else get ready to eat dog food), and then pick among a thousand mutual funds, but then there is the 401(k) plan at work with these Latin American government bond funds and such, and so the only rational response is *not* to create a financial plan."

It doesn't surprise me that he would respond this way, given how inundated we are with countless choices. Even a trip to the grocery store can lead to our feeling overwhelmed and exhausted. I have a friend in New York who lives a few blocks from a fancy mayonnaise store. How many kinds of mayonnaise do we really need? (My friend admits that she's tried numerous flavors, and they're all delicious.)

Of course, things get really frustrating when the stakes are higher than what we're going to put on our BLTs. Take my recent experience with my dog, Zeke. He was having some stomach problems (I'll spare you the details of how I knew), and it was clear we needed to take him to the vet to get him checked out. I'm probably a lot like you: busy. When Zeke got sick, my family was getting ready to leave on vacation, work was piling up, and the kids needed to be shipped back and forth between a bunch of activities.

But luckily the vet is located literally two hundred yards from my office. When I dropped him off, I told the vet I had a ton of errands to run. "Why don't I come back in a few hours once you've had plenty of time to fully check him out?"

When I returned, the vet informed me that they had time to do a full diagnosis and they'd run all kinds of tests.

Then she said, "You have three options."

That was the moment everything fell apart.

As soon as she said "three options," I felt myself start to panic. In fact, I felt like my head was about to explode.

As I tried to collect myself, she started to walk me through option one. About halfway through her description of the treatment, I couldn't take it anymore. I held my hands up in the air, looked her in the eyes, and said, "Stop. Just tell me: If Zeke were your dog, what would you do?"

She went back to walking me through the options. I stopped her again. She did it again: more options.

Finally, I put my finger to my lips and I actually shushed her. Then I said, very slowly, "No. Really. I mean it. Stop giving me options I'm not qualified to evaluate. Please. I'm begging you. . . . Just tell me what to do."

Most financial books and magazines and Web sites are like that vet: they give readers a long list of options that just add to their confusion. No wonder my friend had given up on coming up with a financial plan: he didn't even know where to start.

And he's not the only one. Whether I'm eating dinner with friends or telling someone what I do, the conversation inevitably turns to how hopeless they feel about their retirement or investment plans. More than once, people have asked me the same thing I asked the vet: "Just tell me what to do."

These people are smart. They're great at what they do. Many are total stars in their fields—experts in business, science, and the arts—and yet, when it comes to their own finances, they're stuck. They're often paralyzed by the fear of making the wrong decision.

It doesn't surprise me that my most successful friends are confused when it comes to savings and retirement. When they do something, they want to do it right. They don't just want good advice, they want the *best* advice. They've often got a shelfful of books about investing or finance, but they simply don't have the time to really dive in—so, rather than do the "wrong thing," they do nothing.

Of course, it's not just fear of making a mistake that holds us back from taking action—it's also the mistakes we've already made that we don't want to own up to. Often, just the idea of having to open our bank statements can be stressful so we let them pile up, hoping that something will happen to change our situation. Of course, what actually needs to change is our own behavior—but that's easier said than done.

———

There are many stories these days of people who lost their financial bearings during the housing boom and the crisis that followed—but when I lost my own house in 2010, it was a little bit different.

I'm a financial advisor. I get paid to help people make smart financial choices. I should have known that we couldn't afford a house that cost almost twice what we'd originally set out to spend. I should have known that there was something wrong with being able to borrow 100 percent of the purchase price. I should have listened to my gut when it told me, *Something's wrong.*

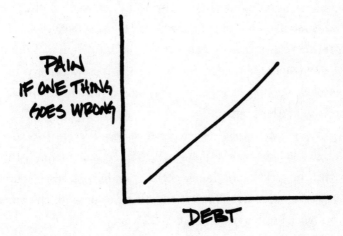

I'm a financial advisor, and yet I never sat down to figure out what it would take to make this work. I just wanted to believe our real estate agent, despite the fact that he was making money on the deal. And it was so easy to believe he had been right, at least at first. We loved our new house. The children went to an awesome public school, and we made some great friends. I could ride my bike to Red Rocks, the wilderness area outside of town. And for a time, the real estate market erased any doubt I may have had.

It just kept going up . . . until, well, you know.

Yes, I'm a financial advisor. But in the heat of the moment, when my income was rising rapidly, when home prices were soaring with no sign of stopping, I wasn't thinking like one.

Some might say I wasn't even thinking at all. I was just following the crowd.

After I watched my house almost triple in value and used some of that equity to start a business, the real estate market collapsed faster than almost any of us realized. Within a matter of just a few short months, we found ourselves faced with the reality that we had to move back to Utah and that we owed more than the house was worth. After working with the bank for almost a year, everybody agreed that a short sale was the best option.

As devastating as that experience was, I learned something valuable: the best financial plan has nothing to do with what the markets are doing, nothing to do with what your real estate agent is telling you, nothing to do with the hot stock your brother-in-law told you about.

It has everything to do with what's most important to you.

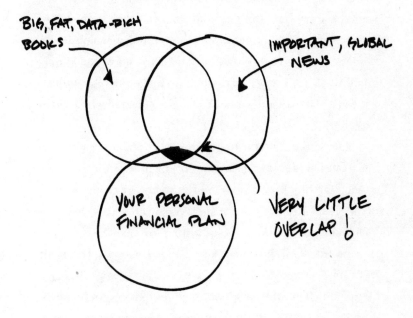

Over the last two decades, I've had thousands of conversations about this topic. I've worked with hundreds of clients to create customized financial plans and talked to hundreds of advisors about their best ideas and techniques. And, as I'll write about throughout this book, I've learned from experience: I've made mistakes that no rational financial advisor should make—but, of course, I'm not just a financial advisor, I'm also human, and a big part of being human involves irrationality.

Irrational decisions and bad calls about money aren't "failures"; they're just what happens when emotional creatures have to make decisions about the future with limited information. They're not something to run from; they're something to be acknowledged, something we can learn from, and, yes, even something we can plan for. With that in mind, we're going to scrap any striving for perfection and instead commit to a process of guessing and making adjustments when things go off track. Of course we're going to make the best guesses we can—but we're not going to obsess over getting them exactly right.

How important is it to get started? "The average working household has virtually no retirement savings" was one of the startling conclusions of a 2013 report from the National Institute on Retirement. "When all households are included—not just households with retirement accounts—the median retirement account balance is $3,000 for all working-age households and $12,000 for near-retirement households. Two-thirds of working households ages fifty-five to sixty-four with at least one earner have retirement savings less than one time their annual income, which is far below what they will need to maintain their standard of living in retirement."[1]

Simply by reading this book and making some choices, you'll be better off than the vast majority of your neighbors.

———

One thing you won't find in this book is a silver bullet investment strategy. There's an entire industry built around the idea that successful financial planning requires finding the best investment: if we just look hard enough or have the right contacts, we'll be able to identify the next hot stock, sector, or mutual fund. However, the research is pretty clear that this strategy almost always leaves us disappointed. We simply aren't great at picking the next Google.

What you will find here is some advice that, at first glance, may seem out of place in a financial planning book. The first three chapters of the book help you think through the kinds of questions and conversations that typically come up when I'm helping my clients create a customized financial plan. Some of them might seem like the kind of questions you'd find in a self-help book, but, I assure you, this isn't a book full of empty promises and trademarked mantras. This is a book about answers.

But here's the thing: your answers shouldn't look anything like my answers or your neighbor's answers. That's why we're going to start with some questions not simply about *how* to save and invest your money, but about *why* you're doing it in the first place.

I know what you want to do: skip to the chapter where I answer the question "Where do I put my money and how much?" Pretty much every client I've ever worked with has walked into my office with an "Okay, kid, show me what you've got" kind of attitude, and to be honest, I was tempted to write that book for you. I could write about how to pick the best stock; I could write a book on "One stock that will change your life." I'd get to be on all the shows, but I wouldn't be helping you. I'd just be adding to the circus. But that's not why I wrote this book. My goal was to help my friend, or my mom, or the friends I've had lunch with.

Am I really supposed to fit my financial plan on one page?

Not long ago, my wife and I were trying to make some really important financial decisions. We'd already spent a lot of time on the details—we'd set up savings accounts, bought insurance, and come up with an investment process. But whenever we had to make a decision, we were getting bogged down in all the details. Finally, out of a sense of frustration, I wondered, "What if I had to put it all on one page? What's the stuff that *really* matters?"

I noticed a Sharpie on my desk and saw card stock in the printer, so I pulled them out and just wrote down the three or four things that were really important to us.

The first answered the question "Why?—Why is money really important to us?" It served as a kind of statement of our values, something that would remind us why we were working hard and saving money.

The remaining three were specific things that we needed to do to reach our major financial goals:

1. We wanted to make sure we fully funded all our retirement accounts each year.
2. We wanted to put a certain amount of money into each of our four kids' education funds each year.
3. All the money we saved beyond that would be set aside in an account to one day buy a house.

That was it.

Then we set it aside.

About a month went by before we found ourselves facing another big decision and having a similar conversation.

TIME WITH FAMILY DOING
    THINGS WE LOVE!

① FULLY FUND ALL RETIREMENT
   ACCOUNTS EACH YEAR

② FUND KIDS' EDUCATION
   ACCOUNT EVERY YEAR

③ SAVE FOR HOUSE

Then I said, "Wait a second. I think we've already done this." So I went and found the one-page plan. After all, we'd already spent the cognitive energy to make these decisions. Why go through them all again?

There's a couple of important things to keep in mind about your one-page plan.

No two financial plans will look the same. Yours will probably look a lot different from the one my wife and I created. That's the point.

What's perhaps most interesting about the one-page plan is what's not on there. What about all the details about how much money you plan to invest each year or how much life insurance to purchase? Don't worry: I'll cover all these topics throughout the book, sharing strategies that will take the complexity out of all these decisions. Your one-page plan simply represents the three to four things that are the most important to you: some action items that need to get done along with a reminder of why you're doing them.

I suggest using a Sharpie for a reason: you can't be too precise with it. Using a thick marker and card stock forces you to make broad statements without worrying too much about how things look. You can't fit very much on a page when you're writing with a Sharpie: this constraint helps you focus on what's really important.

Your goal is not to create a "one-page plan for the rest of your life." Creating a financial plan is a process. My wife and I will look at our plan often—whenever we need to make a big decision, it will be there to guide us—but I'm sure we'll be adjusting it often.

And as we adjust our goals, we'll pull out a new Sharpie and card.

Think about your one-page plan as a snapshot, not an instruction book. If you've ever put together a kids' toy, you'll know that most of them come with a fifty-page instruction manual. Sure, the fifty-page plan is incredibly important—probably vital if you want the drawbridge on the castle to open or the rocket to launch—but what's arguably most important is the picture on the front of the box. The picture lets you know you're on the right track.

Similarly, it's equally important to make choices about your 401(k) allocation and paying down your consumer debt—and I'll walk you through making these kinds of decisions throughout the book—but it's also helpful to keep in mind why you're making all these decisions in the first place. The one-page plan lets you know whether you're on course to meet your goals, or whether you need to make some adjustments.

Remember, *The One-Page Financial Plan* isn't about getting things "right." It's about realizing that you will always get things at least a little wrong. You'll lose the job you thought was secure, you'll take a financial risk that doesn't pan out the way you thought it would, you'll have twins when you were only budgeting for one. In other words: life will happen. I've found it's best to create a financial plan that takes uncertainty as a given—that sets you up to make adjustments as quickly and painlessly as possible so your disappointments won't spiral into disasters.

This book is also about getting really clear about what you want so that you won't be so swayed by your neighbors' new car or ads for that fancy new smart phone—all those "American dream" promises that might have nothing to do with what's most important to you. I've let myself get caught up in those promises, too, so I know how tempting it can be to trade in your own values for the ones that everyone is telling you you should have. But when the paint on the car starts to chip and the gadget gets tossed into the closet with all the others, you can't help but wonder if you've been pouring all your hard-earned money into the wrong things.

Some more good news: none of the foundational work I'm suggesting you do takes very long. In fact, it's the kind of conversation you can have with a spouse or a trusted friend in about an hour. Once you've gone through that

process, I'll switch gears and provide some simple strategies for everything from saving for retirement to rebalancing your 401(k) each year. While I don't believe that any financial plan should be one size fits all, I know that you're busy—and so, I have provided some basic exercises and tips that should help keep your financial plan as simple as possible.

My goal in writing this book is to pull the curtain back a bit: to show you how real financial planning works, to give you an experience of what it's like to work with a real financial advisor. Whether you're working with an advisor or on your own, this book will help you understand the basic steps for creating a personalized plan that takes into account your unique values and goals.

Before we dive in, I want to share a few things I've learned from my two decades as a financial advisor and four decades as an irrational human that I hope you'll keep in mind as you read the book.

One is that the problems are never quite as bad as they seem. When I was at my lowest point—feeling like my decisions had put not only my house and business at risk, but also the happiness of my family—I stopped, took a deep breath, and realized that while many things seemed out of control, I still had the ability to make some changes and set myself on the right track. Today, I rent my house instead of own and live more modestly than I did at the height of the boom, but I'm also really clear on what's important to me: spending time with my family and giving them as many great opportunities as I can.

Another thing I've learned is that we're all in this to-gether. The specifics may vary from person to person and family to family, but most of our money decisions are driven by a desire to feel happy, safe, and secure. Of course, my version of happiness, safety, and security will probably look nothing like my friend's, who has no kids and just wants to have time to travel and pursue her creative goals. So why should my financial plan look like hers?

This is something I try to keep in mind whenever I'm faced with a new financial decision. Since I've shared these ideas with clients and friends, I've watched them realize that the things they thought were impossible—taking time off from work to start a family, spending more time with their small kids, even paying down massive debt—were actually attainable.

Which brings me to a final reason for putting a plan into place:

Creating a financial plan is one of the best ways of giving yourself something that everyone wants more of: time.

Our goal is not to create a one-hundred-page plan that we need to obsess about for hours every day. In fact, quite the opposite: once we've used our one-page plan to guide our decisions about saving and investing, we want to do our best to forget about all those little details, automating processes whenever possible. That way, we won't be tempted to stray from our plan every time the market moves.

I have a friend who sat down and calculated how much time he saves now that he no longer has to pore over financial statements each week. He was shocked to find a whopping four to six hours a week! And not only did he have much more time, by leaving his investments alone, he found they were doing much better. For those of you who think you don't have time to put a plan into place, let me assure you: while it can take a little time to use your one-page plan to guide your financial decisions, by making that small investment, you're setting yourself up to save hundreds of hours each year.

A lot of us think that financial planning is boring and by the numbers—and it can be. But I believe it can actually be a truly exciting and revealing process: it's about realizing the connection between tangible things like the money we make and the intangible things like how great it feels to be there when your daughter scores her first goal.

It's about being really honest about where you want to go, getting really clear about where you are now, and then making your best guesses about how to narrow the gap between the two.

PART ONE
Discovery

THE first step in creating your one-page financial plan is simply to get clear about where you are and where you want to be. When I go through this process with clients, I call it the Discovery meeting—and it's a conversation that can be broken into three parts. Sometimes people go through the Discovery process in as little as an hour. For others, it takes longer.

The good news is, this doesn't require a lot of work, math, or financial savvy. It's actually a relatively simple process. But simple doesn't necessarily mean easy—this discussion brings us face-to-face with our fears about money, and makes it shockingly clear whether or not our behavior lines up with our goals.

Think of this section as the foundational work that will help you create a financial plan that's uniquely suited to your needs: and that means getting to the bottom of what you want from money—and (cue the dramatic music) from your life.

The first chapter consists of an important question. Some people need only about fifteen to twenty minutes to answer it. Others find that some time spent thinking about the question leads them to a deeper answer.

In chapter 2, you'll make some guesses (yes, I said "guesses") about your financial goals and how to meet them.

In chapter 3, you'll get to the place where most financial books might have you begin: by taking stock of where you are today in terms of your finances. This is where most people give up on the process of creating a financial plan. Why? Two reasons: they don't know how to measure their current financial status—and they are often scared of what they'll discover. I'll walk you through the process of creating a "personal balance sheet"—a task typically seen as a major undertaking largely because many traditional financial plans ask for way more information than you could ever know—or that's even useful. Instead, I'll walk you through an exercise that will deliver bottom-line results quickly, focusing on the data that's easily available and most relevant. And perhaps most important, I'll offer some strategies about dealing with the emotional aspects of facing your financial status.

THE MOST IMPORTANT
MONEY QUESTION

A few years ago, while I was working at a large brokerage firm, I sat down to help my friend Sara and her husband, Mark, with their financial plan.

Like so many of my clients, Sara and Mark are smart, successful, and driven. Sara's a managing partner of her emergency group—if you know anything about ER medicine, you know that you've got to be at the top of your game just to get a residency. A rock star in her field and "type A" to the hilt, Sara didn't seem to mind working the long hours required to get ahead. And so it was only natural that when it came to her financial strategy, she didn't want to settle for anything less than the best.

The meeting began as most do. Sara and Mark were hoping I'd share some hot tip or secret. They had an acute problem—they had no idea how to invest the money they'd worked so hard for—and they wanted a solution. But they didn't want just any solution: they wanted the right one.

Instead of rattling off my credentials, my investment strategy, or my thoughts about the current economic landscape, I began the way I start every meeting.

I asked them one question: why is money important to you?

It's a simple enough question, but as Sara and Mark soon discovered, simple questions aren't always so easy to answer.

The Power of "Why?"

After I posed the question, Sara shifted in her seat. She had the same look that almost everyone gets when presented with this question: one that said, "Just *why* exactly are we talking about this? Aren't you supposed to be telling *us* what to do?"

Why is this question so unexpected? Because we're not used to starting financial conversations with a question that might seem more appropriate in a therapy session. We don't go to financial advisors to have touchy-feely conversations about the meaning of life; we want them to tell us where to put our money—and we want them to do it quickly so that we can go back to doing what's important.

Once a few moments passed and Sara and Mark realized that I wouldn't let them move on before they answered, Sara gave the answer most people give when they want to get out of the situation: the easy one.

"Freedom," she said.

Sara's quick response wasn't a surprise. It's a common answer (who doesn't want more freedom?) and a decent enough starting point. But I knew we needed to go deeper. I wrote her answer down on a piece of paper, but pressed her: "What does freedom mean to you?"

At this point, I could tell she was thinking a little harder. Eventually, she answered, "flexibility." I still felt we hadn't gotten anywhere yet, so I asked her to explain. "Okay, so what's important about flexibility?" I asked. "Tell me more."

There was a long pause, and eventually she answered.

"I just want some time."

I remember this moment clearly. I found Sara's answer surprising because she seemed to thrive in a highly competitive environment and nothing she had said gave me the impression that she needed or wanted a break from that lifestyle.

I wrote down "I just want some time" on a piece of paper, but I still didn't feel I understood why time was so important to Sara. So I asked her one last question. "Okay, let's pretend you're there," I said. "Let's say you've gotten to that point where you have more time. What's important about being at that spot?"

After a few minutes of silence, Sara looked at Mark and then responded with some emotion. "I really want to have a family," she said, "and I haven't even had the time to think about it."

The answer surprised Mark. They'd talked about having a family, but he'd never realized how important it was to Sara. This is perhaps not all that shocking—how many of us learn something surprising about our spouses years into our relationships? We're constantly learning new things about the people we love and spend a lot of time with.

But what's so interesting about going through this process is that we learn things about ourselves. In fact, that's what happened with Sara—she even seemed surprised with her own answer. Until we took the moment to have that conversation, she hadn't really made the connection between how hard she was working to earn money and what she hoped her income would bring: the financial security to put the brakes on her high-speed, high-pressure career for a bit so that she could start a family.

"Before we go any further," I said, "is there anything more important than having the freedom and time to start a family?"

"No," she said. "There's nothing more important."

The reason I ask my clients this question is because it helps us understand their values. Often, the process of asking "Why?"—"Why is money important to me?" or "Why have I been so anxious about money lately?" or "Just why do I work so hard anyway?"—uncovers deep desires and fears that we are often too busy or too scared to think about. While the process can be uncomfortable, recognizing what really matters to you is the first step toward making financial decisions that are in sync with your values.

"Great," I said. "So if there's nothing more important, is it okay if we view all your financial decisions through that lens?"

Sara nodded.

Now we were ready to start thinking about a plan.

———

Before you can plan, you have to know why you're planning.

Sara and Mark didn't realize that before I could give them any advice about some future plan, we had to first back up and assess what exactly we were planning *for*. After all, just think how different our strategy would have to have been if what was most important to Sara was expanding her practice or retiring early so that she could write that series of thrillers set in an ER.

Having done this with hundreds of my clients, I've found no more efficient strategy for solving the problem of how to handle our finances than asking "Why is money important to you?"

I first learned a version of this question more than a decade ago from author and speaker Bill Bachrach, and later refined it with help from my mentor, John Bowen. It quickly became my favorite question to start the process of financial planning because it helped uncover the reason why we need to do financial planning in the first place.

Obviously, everyone's answer will be different, but as I've seen firsthand, once you discover it, it flips a hidden switch. Instead of feeling overwhelmed by the supposed complexity surrounding financial decisions, you'll have clarity about which strategies will work best for your particular situation.

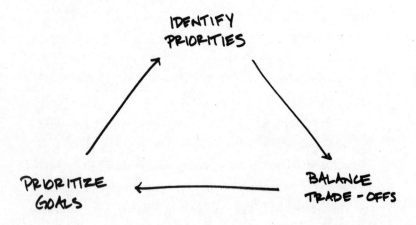

That said, even though this process can be incredibly powerful, it's not always easy. For one thing, it's uncomfortable. We don't like asking ourselves why money is important because it often reflects how we *feel* about money instead of what we *know*. It's much easier (we think) to talk about numbers and cents than about our emotions and deep desires.

And it's scary to take this dive into the unknown. What if the answer changes everything we thought we knew about money—and maybe even everything we thought we wanted out of life?

To understand why this Discovery process is critical, let's switch to another area of your life for a moment. Let's say you weren't feeling well but you didn't know why. You'd make an appointment with your doctor and explain your symptoms. How would you feel if, twenty-seven seconds after you'd listed your symptoms, the doctor began writing you a prescription? Or, even worse, before you finished speaking, she concluded that you probably have the same flu as everyone else?

Compare that with finding a doctor who really takes the time to diagnose you properly. This doctor examines you and gives you tests before making a diagnosis or giving you a prescription.

Which one would you prefer? Obviously you'd feel better with the doctor who took the time to walk through the diagnosis process. You shouldn't expect anything different from your financial life.

Asking why money is important to you is a bit like applying

the rigor of a doctor's examination to your financial health. It's no crazier than going to the doctor's office for a checkup *before* you get a prescription.

The process looks a bit like this:

A. You're noting your symptoms (your financial life feels out of balance or just needs a checkup).

B. You're identifying what health would look like (you're asking yourself why money is important).

C. You're discovering a solution (you're using the values you've identified to drive your financial planning decisions).

Logically, we know that doing the last thing first—asking a financial advisor for a solution before identifying the problem—makes no sense, yet that's where the traditional financial services industry would have us start: at the end.

DIAGNOSIS ⟶ PRESCRIPTION

↑

START HERE!

I'm encouraging you to instead start at the beginning. Then you can use what you've learned about your values to come up with a financial plan that's right for you.

Keep Asking "Why?"

By now, the importance of asking why money is important to you should be clear. Having an understanding of your values can help you make better financial decisions—not better because they reflect some Wall Street strategy, better because they're tailor-made for you.

Take some time now to follow the same process that Sara and I went through by asking yourself why money is important to you. You can go do this alone, but you might also find it useful to ask a trusted friend to sit down with you; he or she may be able to see patterns or habits that you cannot. If you're doing this with a spouse, it's important that each partner answer the question separately. If money is important to you for different reasons, you want to find that out as soon as possible. (Later in this chapter, I'll share some tips about how to have important money conversations with spouses and family members.)

I recommend starting with the big question: "Why is money important to me?" but you might find that other "Why?" questions will help you home in on an answer that's clear and specific.

Ask yourself:

- *Why do I invest so much of my money and time on* X?

- *Why do I spend so little on* Y *when I claim it's so important?*

- *Why do I save as much (or as little) as I do? What am I hoping to achieve?*

Like Sara's, your answers may start out vague—many of my clients start with big ideas like "freedom" or "security" or "control." I encourage you to keep going until you hit upon the concrete reasons behind these somewhat intangible concepts. Strive for specifics like "I want my children to have more opportunities than I did" or "I want more time to volunteer in my community" or "I don't want to have to worry about money like my parents did."

If you hit a dead end when it comes to figuring out what's most important to you, there are two places to look that should give you a clue:

- *How you spend your time*

- *How you spend your money*

That's why the old saying "The calendar and the checkbook never lie" resonates with so many of us. It turns out the way we spend our money and our time often says something about what we value.

TIME SPENT
+ MONEY SPENT
_____
= WHAT YOU REALLY VALUE

A caveat: while the calendar and the checkbook are good places to start, remember that you might also be surprised to discover that you've been spending a lot of time and money on things that don't really matter—at the expense of the things that do. This process can help you reset the balance.

Because we're entering unknown and potentially scary territory, I suggest you set up a few guardrails to make this process productive.

Before you ask "Why?":

1.   Set aside a time.

Whether you're beginning this process alone or with a spouse, it's important to carve out the time to ask "Why?" Pick a time when you'll have the energy—avoid late nights or the end of a long week. Often, it won't take a ton of time to figure out why money matters to you, but you'll want to leave yourself enough time to reflect and deal with any surprising revelations the process may have helped you uncover.

2.   Get out of the house.

I used to joke with my clients that someone was going to cry in our first meeting and it wasn't going to be me. In fact, a good way to tell that you haven't gone deep enough is if you haven't gotten emotional. For this reason, I advise picking a place outside of your normal routine—it could be a café you don't usually go to or your CPA's office or a private room at your local library. Having a specific place can serve as a reminder that these conversations can be emotional, and can help you prepare for that. For the same reason, I suggest keeping conversations about money out of the bedroom, the park where you go to relax, or the place where you had your first date.

3. Let go of the past.

I recently worked with a couple, Caitlin and James, who lost a large amount of money in the stock market. While the bad investment was the result of poor timing, not poor judgment, Caitlin just couldn't let it go. Every time the subject of money came up, she couldn't help but point out that they would have far more money if it weren't for that mistake.

If we approach the process with the right frame of mind, reflecting on our mistakes may help us avoid repeating the same mistake in the future. But at a certain point, you need to make peace with what's happened in the past and move on. This is especially crucial when you're assessing what's important to you. Don't use the mistakes you've made in the past as an excuse to deny yourself what's really important.

4. Adopt a "no shame, no blame" attitude.

When my wife and I first discussed moving to Park City, Utah, we looked at a building lot. It cost more than we felt comfortable spending, so we didn't buy it. When we finally moved a few years later, we learned that the lot was for sale again. But this time around, it was five times more expensive!

It would have been easy for each of us to blame the other for missing that opportunity. In fact, it's right across the street from a park we go to a couple of times a week—just think of all those opportunities to get bummed out about our decision. . . . Rather than let it serve as a constant reminder of our mistake, though, we just sort of look at each other when we pass it, acknowledging that it's not worth the frustration. Besides, the lot was still more expensive than we could have afforded at the time, a fact we could easily forget if we get caught up in the blame game.

We all have made financial mistakes in the past. By adopting a "no shame, no blame" attitude, we can reframe mistakes as valuable lessons. Over time, they'll lose the emotional charge.

5. Skip over goals—for now.

The purpose of asking "Why?" isn't to come up with specific goals or plans of action. It's meant to reveal the *reason* why you have certain goals. Expect the first answers to come fairly easily. But give yourself time to pause and really think; by doing so, you can go even deeper, getting much closer to what's most important.

Remember, this process was designed to make you uncomfortable. You will no doubt recognize some inconsistencies between your values and your behavior. Don't worry. We all do. That's just part of the process of trying to live a more aligned life. But that's the point—once you've hit upon what's most important to you, you'll have a tool for these decisions going forward. These conversations often involve someone else, so it's important to give your partners or family members the space to talk about money without fear of judgment.

Once you've hit upon your "most important thing," you'll have a tool that will help you make lots of decisions going forward—and not simply decisions that seem financial in nature. Knowing your values can make it easy to say no to things that distract us from what's most important. As best-selling author Stephen Covey said, "It's easy to say 'no!' when there's a deeper 'yes!' burning inside."

Asking "Why?" helps you identify that "deeper yes."

Why We Fight About Money—and What to Do About It

Years ago, my wife and I had dinner with another couple, Bob and Sue. During the meal, we were talking about money, the market, and our goals and dreams for our families. As we were talking about what's important to us, Sue spoke up. "I really want the flexibility to travel more."

Bob looked shocked. "What? I never knew that," he said. "I love to travel but I didn't think that was important to you at all."

What made this exchange so surprising is that Bob and Sue had been married for more than a decade in a solid relationship. All the signs pointed to their having had this conversation, but they hadn't, and there was an awkward moment as the disconnect sank in. After an uncomfortable silence, we looked at one another and laughed. Isn't it funny how we can be in a relationship with someone for fifteen years and not know such an important detail? Laughter aside, this moment was really valuable. It helped Sue and Bob change the way they'd been thinking about the next thirty or forty years.

I've touched on why this process can be so challenging, but if you're married or have kids, this discussion can rocket straight past uncomfortable to unbearable. Few families sit down and have even the most basic of conversations about what money means to their family—or they wait until they're forced to have a discussion because of some financial setback. As a result, they may find out they have completely different ideas about the future.

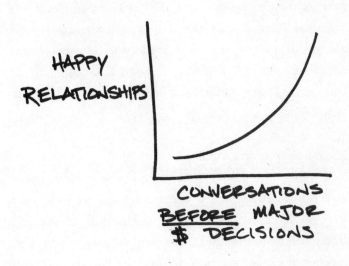

HAPPY RELATIONSHIPS

CONVERSATIONS BEFORE MAJOR $ DECISIONS

More than once, I've been in client meetings where it's clear that couples are having their first discussion about big decisions—their kids' education, their saving strategies, their thoughts about retirement. Without fail, either one or both individuals are surprised, if not shocked, by their partner's opinion on a topic. To help you navigate this discussion, I suggest keeping a few things in mind:

1. **It's almost impossible to overestimate money's role in our relationships.**

Take a quick mental count of how many arguments you've had that involve money. It's probably quite a few. Even if the argument wasn't explicitly about money, it's a driving factor for many family disagreements. So don't be surprised if your significant other doesn't immediately understand or appreciate how important your values are to you. It may take some time, but commit to following through with the discussion because it's all but impossible to remove money from a relationship.

2. **We all have baggage.**

Each of us brings a set of deeply ingrained beliefs, habits, and feelings about money to our relationships. Most of us were raised in families where money (like religion and politics) was a subject not to be discussed in polite company. As a result, we have very little training on how to talk about and deal with the emotional issues inherent in our financial lives.

Don't be afraid to defend what you've said is important to you, but understand that a spouse or child may not see it the same way. The goal is to stay respectful and look for common ground (remember: "no shame, no blame").

3. **Know when to talk about money—and when to table the conversation.**

Spontaneous conversations about why money is important can either be the best you'll ever have or the worst. If you're walking around in your local park on a beautiful spring day and realize that maybe you could spend some time off rediscovering your own city rather than taking an expensive trip abroad, that can be a perfect time to open a discussion about what truly matters. If you just got home from a long day at work and realized your Amex bill is a lot higher than you anticipated, that might be a time to table the conversation for a moment when you're feeling clear and fresh.

4. Money seems to be the last thing we talk about (at least at first).

It's not unusual if you didn't talk about money during your courtship or engagement. Many believe that if you need to talk about money in your relationship, it's a sign you're not truly in love. Prenuptial agreements are passé, and no one wants to be accused of marrying just for the money.

But even if you've managed to avoid any money discussions before marriage, you can't avoid them forever. The sooner you sit down and talk about why money is important to each of you, the sooner you can work together toward reconciling competing visions of the future.

Remember, these conversations can be uncomfortable; because of that, having this conversation on your own can be challenging and you may benefit from having an objective third party present. We'll talk about that later in the book.

Financial Planning Is About More Than Money

As I mentioned earlier, I consider my family to be my highest priority; I work as hard as I do because I want the financial freedom to be able to spend time with my four children and give them a foundation for a life full of opportunity.

Sounds great, right? Sure, at least until those weeks where I spend hours on Twitter trying to bring attention to my ideas. Watching the number of retweets soar seems like concrete proof that I'm doing something positive for my career—and therefore related to my values—until I catch myself interrupting a conversation with my thirteen-year-old son to check if someone had responded to a tweet.

During the process of asking yourself why money is important, I expect you'll discover that there are different kinds of "human capital." Most financial planning focuses primarily on money while ignoring three other incredibly valuable things:

1. Your time
2. Your skills
3. Your energy

But as I'm sure you already know, these other three are equally important.

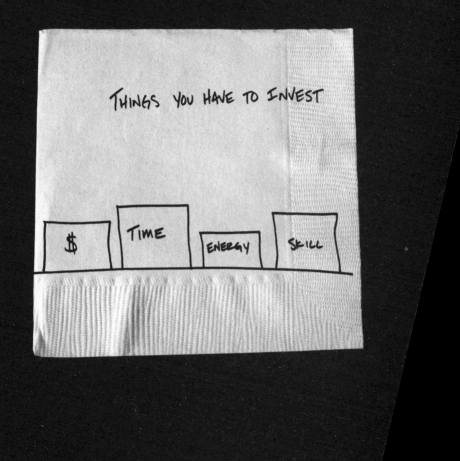

Realizing I was taking time away from my son to tweet served as a great reminder that I needed to stop thinking about capital just in terms of money. Sure, getting people on Twitter buzzing about my work might help me financially, but in this case, the cost of using Twitter to advance my work was too great for me personally.

It may help to think about the different kinds of human capital in units—units of time, units of energy, and so on. Each day, you take some of your units and exchange them for units of money. You then take those units of money and spend them on something. But every time you exchange a unit, there's a trade-off, and we often fail to look past the immediate return to the potential long-term consequences. When we think about money only in terms of dollars and cents, we risk depleting our stores of energy, time, and skill.

Of course, there will be times when our reserves of all four kinds of capital will be well stocked, allowing us to do more of the things we want. Other times, our needs and wants will seem to dwarf the limited resources we have to throw at them. Identifying your values by asking what's important to you can help you cut out the activities that may bring in monetary income but pull you away from what's truly important in your life.

I've been amazed to see how people's lives have been transformed once they figure out how to manage their human capital. They worry a lot less about things they have no control over. They stop caring about society's ideas of what they're supposed to need, and concentrate on what's really important. They spend more time with the people they love and doing things that make them happy.

Focus on What You Can Control

When I ask clients, "Why is money important to you?" many of them say, "I just want to be in control" or "I want financial security." Their answers don't surprise me. Each day, we're confronted with lots of big, bad news about big, bad things that will surely lead to the end of the world. The problem? We have no control over lots of things, making it very easy to feel we lack control over *anything*.

I remember feeling this way in 2008. I was living in Las Vegas, about to lose my home, and I felt like my business was going to disappear at any moment, too. Some nights, I would watch the Tokyo Stock Exchange open and then stay up to watch London wake up—and I was not even a trader. I just hoped to see some sign of relief. Most nights none came, and I never made it to bed.

When I could actually fall asleep, my dreams were disturbing and unsettling. In one recurring nightmare, I would find myself sitting alone in a room with an oversized light switch on the wall. It had the name of my business above it and the words ON and OFF. An evil-looking guy in a suit would come in, grab the switch, and, laughing maniacally, flip it from ON to OFF.

Nothing I did could change my feeling that things were spiraling out of control.

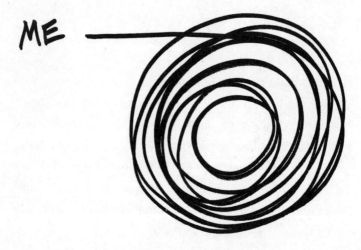

But then something did change. It might sound like something out of a yoga class, but I remembered a friend telling me that when you feel anxious and out of control, it helps to focus on breathing.

So I did. Every time my mind started to latch on to one of these problems, I would focus on my breathing, one breath at a time. There were a few days where it seemed like all I could do was go from one breath to the next, but doing so helped me gain a *tiny* sense of control.

Nothing about my financial situation had changed, but over time, that tiny sense of control grew. After a while, it became easier to focus again on the things that I had some control over and the things that mattered. An evening out with my wife, time with my kids, going for a long bike ride were simple things, but by focusing on them, I realized that a lot of the other things didn't matter.

I soon found myself able to do something about my situation. By focusing only on what I could control, and letting go of the rest, everything changed.

The news was still just as crazy, but I let it go.

The markets were still just as scary, but I let it go.

It just takes a small step—or a breath, if you will. And from there, you can feel a little more in control and break that cycle of panic and fear.

When you find yourself obsessing over the same issues time after time, remind yourself that no matter how bad things seem, you can gain control and clarity by remembering what matters most. It will help you focus on the things you have some control over, and let go of the things you don't.

It can take time to figure out what's really important.

I started this chapter with Sara and Mark's story because we were able to answer "Why?" in just a few minutes, but don't be surprised if it takes you more than four questions to get your own answer. Sara's answer popped up fast because it had been sitting just below the surface for quite some time. Yours may be buried a little deeper. Give yourself time. And give yourself permission to think about money in new ways—don't forget to factor in other forms of capital: time, energy, and skills.

And last, but definitely not least, remember to ignore any one-size-fits-all financial advice that starts with a solution. Your goal is to create a financial plan that's right for you—so why not start by thinking about what you really want to achieve?

Your One-Page Financial Plan

If you haven't done so already, take out your own Sharpie and a piece of paper, and jot down your answers to the question "Why is money important to me?" Your answer or answers will reflect the values that are most important to you—they should be at the top of your one-page plan.

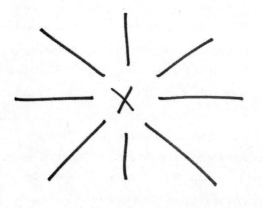

...WHERE DO YOU WANT TO GO?

In the chapters that follow, I'll walk you through the process of setting some goals in line with those values. Together, your values and goals will help you create a one-page plan that will guide all your financial decisions: from how much to save for retirement to customizing a unique investment portfolio.

2.

GUESS WHERE YOU WANT
TO GO

WHEN it comes to talking about our financial futures, the one thing we're most scared of is uncertainty.

Few of us think we should be able to predict major world events or know what our kids will want to be when they grow up, but for some reason, we think we're supposed to have a crystal ball when it comes to our financial futures.

Ironically, some traditional approaches to financial planning can make our fear of uncertainty even worse. If you've ever gone to a financial advisor's office and gone through the process of setting goals, you've probably noticed the obsession with a false sense of precision. We get hit with questions like "I need to know what your utility bills are twenty-five years from now" or "Tell us how much you plan to spend on auto insurance in 2043."

For this reason, many of us put off financial planning altogether. "Forget about a financial planner," we think. "They're just going to have me generate another two-hundred-page book of plans; the last time I did that, it sat on my shelf for two years and I never looked at it once."

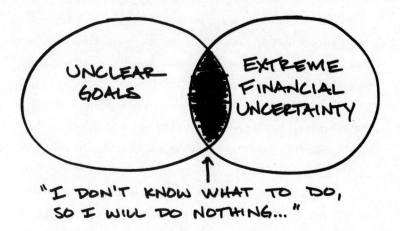

"I DON'T KNOW WHAT TO DO, SO I WILL DO NOTHING..."

Rather than tell you that you should start setting some goals, I'm going to tell you something you might not have heard before:

Relax.

Look, there's nothing wrong with setting two short-range goals, two mid-range goals, and one big, hairy, audacious goal when it comes to your finances. But it's also not necessary. Nor are time lines or deadlines or any other kinds of lines: life doesn't often follow the linear path we expect it to—rather than let that freak us out, we can embrace that uncertainty and work with it.

The point of financial planning is not to cling to a false sense of security that you'll know where you'll be in thirty or forty years—because you won't. Plans change, the unexpected occurs, and we all know the John Lennon quote about life happening when we were busy making other plans.

I like to think of financial goal setting like I'm planning a freewheeling vacation to Europe. Rather than sticking to a by-the-minute agenda, you'd probably do better with a plan that leaves room for the unexpected: that way, you can choose to take the walking tour on the sunniest day of your trip, and you'll have time to have a piece of cake at the charming restaurant you couldn't have found in any of your travel books.

I'm not talking about throwing out your plans altogether, but rather suggesting you give yourself some wiggle room to make decisions on the fly: after all, you might find that the Leaning Tower of Pisa isn't all it's cracked up to be—it's crowded and full of people selling souvenirs—wouldn't you rather have a loose enough plan so that you can ditch the crowds and head to the countryside for an afternoon instead?

A lot of my work with clients is about finding the balance between two extreme approaches to financial planning. On the one hand, we all know those people who tape their financial goals to their rearview mirrors to remind themselves daily of exactly what they need to do to meet their goals. But that's never seemed like a fun way to live to me. And from my experience, it doesn't seem to work.

And then there's the opposite camp that says, "I'm just going to live for today and not care about goals." And we all know where that approach leads us.

In my personal experience and my work with clients, I've found that people have had the most success when they abandon those two extreme approaches and instead admit that when it comes to the future, they don't know exactly what will happen.

But they can make some good guesses about where they'd like to go.

Don't be committed to the *guess*, be committed to the *process of guessing*.

As scary as "I don't know" sounds, I've found that there is a tremendous sense of freedom that comes with recognizing that we just don't know what the future will look like. Most of us don't know what industry we'll be working in next year, let alone how much we'll be able to save over the next three decades or how much we'll need to spend once we've retired.

It can take time to accept just how uncertain the future is—if you're having trouble, ask yourself if your life today looks exactly how you would have predicted it five or ten years ago. Maybe the big-picture stuff looks the same— you're living in Boston or Charleston as you had always hoped—but how could you ever have predicted your smart phone bills a decade before the advent of the iPhone? Or how much real estate prices would fluctuate in the last ten years? Or that the cost of college tuition would triple over the last forty years?[1]

Accepting that we just don't know exactly how things will turn out allows us to let go of any anxiety around the idea that we should be able to predict the future—or that we should at least find someone who can. Let me share a secret with you about that: There isn't anyone who knows what the next week, month, year, or even decade of the stock market will look like. And if an advisor or investment expert tells you they can: run.

It's tempting to believe that there's someone out there who can rescue us from our uncertainty, someone with sophisticated enough algorithms or a brilliant enough research staff. But there isn't. Sure, experts can model the direction of the economy based on historical data, but as we learn every time a bubble bursts or the market crashes, often the experts are wrong.

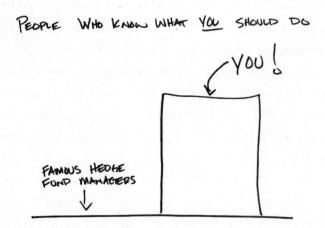

Once we've accepted that a lot can happen between now and the future, financial planning boils down to making the best guess we can about what goals will help us live the life we want. Don't worry about getting it "right." You can—and should—simply course-correct your guess when you notice yourself going off track.

Unfortunately, most people are so afraid of making the

wrong guess, they don't guess at all. It reminds me a bit of a conversation between Alice and the Cheshire Cat:

> "Would you tell me, please, which way I ought to go from here?"
>
> "That depends a good deal on where you want to get to," said the Cat.
>
> "I don't much care where," said Alice.
>
> "Then it doesn't matter which way you go," said the Cat.
>
> "—so long as I get somewhere," Alice added as an explanation.
>
> "Oh, you're sure to do that," said the Cat, "if you only walk long enough."

Like Alice, we all want to end up somewhere, but we increase our chances of getting to a place we actually want to *be* by making a choice.

Guessing can be a frustrating process, since it involves making some really important decisions under extreme uncertainty. We have to guess what the markets will do in ten years, where interest rates will be in twenty, and how much utilities will cost at a time when the utilities we use today will look like something out of *The Flintstones*. Even more difficult, we have to get inside the head of someone who's a complete stranger to us today: ourselves in thirty or forty years.

Regardless of all the uncertainty and assumptions, it's still important to take a guess at our goals. Otherwise, we'll be like Alice, asking for directions without knowing what directions we need.

So how do we know which directions we need? We begin with what's important.

Guessing Your Way to Your Goal

You've just thought quite a bit about your values. You've had a conversation about why money is important with a spouse, trusted friend, or advisor. Those values will serve as the lens through which you can view your entire financial plan.

Now we're going to switch gears slightly and talk about goals, keeping in mind that the set of core values you identified in the last chapter can be useful not only in helping you nail down some goals, but also in helping you prioritize goals when we start ranking them later in the chapter.

Chances are, you already have a few goals in mind—but they're probably a little broad or undefined. It's time to put a framework around your answers to make them more concrete and actionable. Here's how Sara and Mark, the couple whose story I introduced in chapter 1, mapped out some of their goals.

"Let's start with an easy one," I said, after Sara revealed that one of her most important goals was starting a family. "What would it take to get to the place you want to be?"

"Well," she said, "I'm going to have to work less. And in order to feel comfortable doing that, a couple of things would need to fall into place. My partners at the medical center would need to be okay with me taking some time off, Mark would need to be okay with it, and I would need to be okay with it."

"And what would 'okay' mean?"

I suspect that Sara already knew the answer to this question. In my experience, most people have a pretty good idea of what they'd need to meet some financial goal—often, they have a specific number in mind, even if they've never really done the math to get there. By taking a guess, we can see if our "number" is a good estimate, or if we need to make some adjustments.

"Well," said Sara, "we'd need to feel like we're on track for retirement." To be clear, it wasn't that Sara expected to have met all her retirement goals before starting her family. She just wanted to make sure she was on track for meeting them decades later, and that taking the time off wouldn't make those goals impossible to reach.

I asked Sara what that would look like. "I love my work," she said, "but by age fifty-five, I'd like to choose whether or not I have to work. By sixty-five, I might not be able to work in an ER anymore, so I'd like to retire."

So I asked her, "If you were to retire today, how much money would you need per month to live the way you'd hoped?"

Sara gave me the number, and we wrote it down.

"That's your first goal," I said. "To make sure you're on track today to hit that retirement goal in the future."

Then I continued, "What else is important right now?"

At that point, we were able to circle back to the first conversation about what was most important. In addition to starting a family, Sara and Mark had told me that they liked to take one big trip every summer. We calculated the cost and then added it to the list of goals.

Next, we talked about setting aside an emergency fund for about three to six months, and we added that to the list.

You may be surprised to discover that the "number" you had in mind for your goal was way off base. Many of my clients, in fact, have discovered that they overestimated the amount they'd need to achieve some goal. This can be tricky; if you're an insecure person, no amount of money is going to make you feel secure. But sometimes walking through this process can help you see you were making a goal seem unattainable by inflating the numbers needed to get there.

Your Goals May Surprise You

Often, your goals can come as quite a surprise. This is why I suggest you not limit yourself when it comes to this portion of the exercise. We'll get to prioritization later. For now, allow yourself to really ask "What if?" You may be surprised to find that many of your seemingly unattainable goals are actually quite reasonable.

This was certainly true with my clients Henry and Elizabeth. As often is the case, they were not only clients but also good friends. Henry, a doctor, and Elizabeth, a full-time mom, have three kids—and at the time we met, their oldest couldn't have been more than eight or nine. We didn't have to talk long for it to become clear that gaining some financial security for their kids was important to Henry and Elizabeth.

And so, they said, setting up education accounts would naturally be a part of their financial plan. But as I dug deeper into why this was the most important thing, something else came up.

Henry and Elizabeth felt that in America, we've got the wrong idea about how to spend our time and money. They hated the idea of working really hard when the kids are young in the hopes of having a relationship with them in high school. "When they're teenagers, they could have purple hair and nose rings," said Henry. (We can cut Henry some slack for sounding uptight; this was a decade ago.) "They're not going to even want to talk to us!"

"What we'd really like," they told me, "is to take six months off and drive in an RV around the country and home-school our kids."

I asked Henry and Elizabeth if this goal was reasonable. Could Henry take the time off from work? Could they save up enough for a six-month sabbatical?

They thought about it before answering. "I think we could," they agreed.

"If you could do it," I said, "*would you?*"

I remember they got a kind of deer-in-the-headlights look in their eyes. They'd never thought the dream was a realistic one; it was just the kind of "What if?" game you played on vacations or over a nice dinner. But they had just said that time with their kids was the most important thing. Suddenly, an idea that always seemed impossible sounded like the very reason they'd been working so hard.

"Yeah," they said, finally. "I think we would."

The thought that they could make this vision real was a huge "Whoa!" moment for Henry and Elizabeth. They turned a vague dream into a concrete goal, putting it down on paper that they wanted to travel around the country. Next, we began the process of calculating how much it would cost.

Three Guesses for Determining What Your Goals Are— and How Much They'll Cost

Henry and Elizabeth weren't certain about how much their six-month vacation would cost, but they could begin to tally up the cost of RV, gas, food, insurance, school supplies, and discretionary expenses and make a pretty good guess.

When it comes to determining the cost of your goals, you can throw the need for precision out the window. You'll still be better off than most people just by making your best guess. Let's say you decided in the last chapter that what was most important to you was "providing your kids with the financial security you didn't have growing up." You can use that answer to come up with some financial goals such as:

- *We'd like to save enough to send our kids to state college.*

- *We'd like to set up an emergency fund for three to six months.*

Then you can start listing some other goals you know will need to be addressed. They can be short-, medium-, or long-term goals (remember, you're just guessing):

- *I can see the car will need to be replaced in five years.*

- *We want to retire by age sixty-five.*

- *We want to pay down our mortgage in twenty years.*

And finally, don't forget some stretch goals that might not be at the top of the list, but which may be closely related to your values—such as the desire to give your kids some of the opportunities you never had.

- *We'd like to take a small family trip each summer.*

- *We'd like to help our kids for the first one or two months after school while they look for a job.*

Some of those costs will be easy to calculate. But how do we put a number to those that won't be?

Take saving up for retirement, a key goal for nearly everyone I've ever worked with. If you try to get it "right," this process could make your head spin. You may avoid the exercise altogether for fear of getting it wrong. A simpler approach is to just guess. One way to get there is to ask: if you lost your job and had to live off your savings, how much would you spend every month? Stated as a goal, that would look like:

> *By the time I'm sixty, I'd like to be able to have a retirement income of $7,500 per month.*

Or take an emergency fund, which I recommend that all my clients set up whenever "security" comes up in our first conversations. Most people are more than fine with a fund that will protect them for six months or so, but three months may be fine if you're a tenured professor at a university, while twenty-four months may not be enough if you're a serial entrepreneur. Everyone's idea of security is a little different; if you're quiet and listen to your inner voice, I bet you already have some sense of what will work for you.

Here's a "three-guess process" for estimating how much your goals will cost. Once you've guessed at each goal, take another guess about when you'd like to achieve it, and how much it will cost. This process won't make the future any less certain, but it will help ensure that you're ready for the things you'd like to have happen, and prepared for the inevitable challenges that will arise from time to time.

1. What is the goal?
2. When do you want to do it?
3. How much will it cost?

Still not sure? Remember: You're just guessing. That said, you should still make your guesses the best you can. Be specific.

Just saying "I want my kids to be financially secure" isn't enough of a goal. "I want my kids to be able to go to a private university if they want" is a way of making that goal more concrete.

A WISH

A GOAL

"I'll save money each month for my travel fund" is a good starting point. But "I'll find $100 on the fifteenth of each month" is better.

Even though I'm asking you to be specific, give yourself permission to be flexible. An attitude of flexibility goes a long way toward dealing with uncertainty. There is something very powerful about having specific goals but not obsessing about them.

Your Values Can Serve as a System of Checks and Balances

It's time to return to your Sharpie and piece of paper. Underneath your answer to the question "Why is money important to me?" you can begin writing down your guesses.

Once you write down all your guesses, begin ranking each goal in terms of importance and urgency. Sometimes you will have to deal with something that is urgent, like paying off a credit card bill, before you can move on to long-term goals, like saving for retirement. When you have to weigh different goals against one another, use the values you identified in chapter 1 to guide you in the prioritization process. That doesn't mean if you've identified time with your family as a core value that you're not going to have to work hard to fund your other goals. What it does mean is using your values to guide each decision so that you're making these decisions consciously. There are always going to be trade-offs.

As we started looking at all the goals Sara and Mark

came up with, it became clear that putting aside thousands of dollars a year to travel was bumping up against their most important goal: having the time to start a family.

"Which one will you choose?" I asked them.

Since starting a family was the most important thing, the answer was a no-brainer, and they were able to tweak their original goal, opting for a less expensive vacation or even skipping trips until they were able to save a significant amount for Sara's time off.

This process can be eye-opening: it allows us to see whether our goals are in line with our values. I remember a client who insisted that more than anything else, he just wanted to be the best dad. When we got to the process of listing goals, many of them surrounded having more time with his kids, but there were naturally some others. "I really want to buy an M5," he said, referring to a BMW that, at the time, clocked in at $80,000.

We added it to the list, but when we got to the process of ranking goals, I reminded him that this secondary goal would make it harder for him to do what was most important. "Wait a second—do you really want to have to put in any extra time at work to have the money for the car?"

I reminded him of his values not out of judgment. We want to remember the "No shame, no blame" rule when list-ing our values and goals. We're simply pointing out places where our goals and values might not be aligned. Often, my clients are shocked to realize that they've been pouring money into an area that wasn't truly important at the expense of things that were; going through this process reminds us our money wells are not unlimited—we might think we're treating ourselves by indulging in the moment, but it's often at the expense of the more important stuff down the line.

Of course, staying committed to your most important values is easier said than done. Who hasn't made really important New Year's resolutions that they abandoned by the third week of January? The point is to stay as aware as we can when temptation strikes. And strike it will. We don't often think that money spent on a new car can be directly translated into time not spent with our kids—but when we forget to make room for the intangible things in our financial planning, we pay the price.

Stop Obsessing over Your Goals

As important as it is to go through this process of "goal guessing," it's equally important to let go of the need to obsess over your goals. The first time my wife and I ever made a list of financial goals, something like fifteen years ago, we actually lost track of the paper. The following year, when the topic came up, we went looking for the paper and found it tucked away in a drawer. And here's the amazing thing: we had totally forgotten about the items on our list, and yet we had achieved every one of the short-term goals on the list—even very specific goals, such as spending a week in Costa Rica.

We weren't sitting around obsessing over our goals. When a decision needed to be made, we didn't go searching for the list. And yet somehow, we achieved what we'd hoped we would.

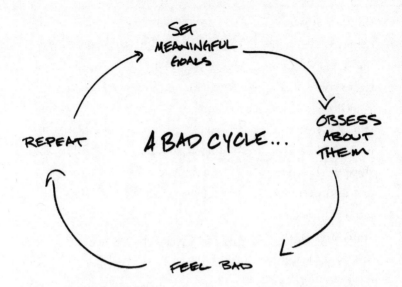

There's No Such Thing as Perfect

Given the amount of time in each day and the number of resources we have at our disposal, it's only natural that we have an expectation that we're going to get the decisions we make about money "perfect." But there's a problem with getting caught up in the idea of perfect: things change.

Whether we like it or not, our lives are in a constant state of flux. Just as we adapt to things like relationships coming to an end or having a new baby, we need to adapt to changes surrounding money.

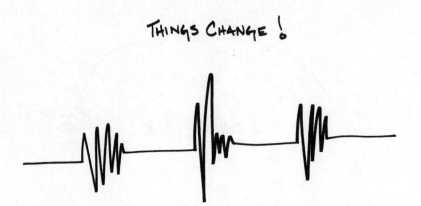

THINGS CHANGE!

If you or your partner loses your job, you need to adjust how much you can save each month. If your plans to have another child get moved ahead a year or two, you may need to buy a new car sooner than you planned. Your goal to retire early may be put on hold after a health emergency. In each example, you didn't do anything wrong; life just happened.

Few financial decisions should be set in stone. At some point, we'll all need to recalibrate, taking into account new circumstances that change our decisions. Too often we get caught up in thinking that this recalibration is a sign we made a mistake.

Hardly. We just have a life.

In fact, if you don't ever find yourself recalibrating your decisions, you're likely ignoring some issues that might become problems down the line.

Remember that you're not simply going to guess once and hope that you got it right: this is an ongoing process. Your guesses will change—because life changes. That knowledge can do one of two things: (1) stop you in your tracks, or (2) free you to start somewhere.

It's your choice which option you pick.

Sometimes We'll Be Disappointed

Not long ago, a woman contacted me after I did an art show in her city and asked me for some financial planning advice. As we talked about what was important to her, it was clear she was really hung up on her "bucket list." She'd always wanted to travel to Nepal and spend a fair bit of time there. But she hadn't been able to do it and now that she was in her early sixties, it was becoming more obvious that she might never get the chance. With tears in her eyes, she told me she finally realized that she might never have the money or the time to accomplish everything on her list.

Yet, just moments before, we had talked about her job as a docent at the local art museum, which was a source of incredible satisfaction. She lived near a trail and got to walk her dog there every morning, and had family nearby with whom she had close relationships.

I could see this was very emotional for her, but at a certain point, I stopped her. "Hold on," I said. "Look at all the stuff that's really gone well." She lived a life that many would consider a dream. She participated in her community and enjoyed meaningful work. But despite all that, it was clear from our conversation that the pain of her unmet expectations was very real.

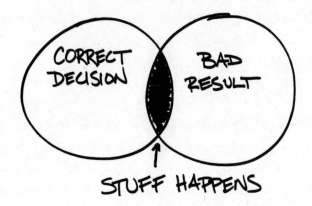

No matter how good our guesses, we may have to confront a hard truth: we won't have enough money to reach all of our goals.

There are few things more painful than working hard for something that might be just out of reach. But this, too, is also part of life. We learn to deal with disappointments, set more attainable goals, and move on.

For some, this disappointment comes when we realize that the retirement we planned is no longer an option. Years of working and saving just didn't turn out the way we'd hoped. So it's no surprise that if we spent a decade or two attached to a certain outcome, even delaying life because we're so focused on that outcome, we're really disappointed when it doesn't happen.

The question is: What do we do about it? Can we avoid feeling disappointed?

I think we can, but to do so, we have to do something a little radical. We've all heard the stories of people who were completely focused on goals like retiring by age sixty or having $1,750,000 in the bank—they might reach them, but when they look back, they see a trail littered with broken relationships. What many of these stories share is that disappointments often come when people are so focused on outcomes that they miss out on life. They lack the flexibility they need to adjust their goals as different circumstances arise. As part of figuring out your guesses, I suggest thinking seriously about letting go of outcome-based goals and focusing instead on the process of living the lives we want right now.

1. Let go of expectations about the future.

Just in case life hasn't already shown you otherwise, the world doesn't necessarily owe you anything. Making guesses about our goals can set us on the right track. But don't turn a guess into an expectation. Recognize that circumstances might arise that derail even those goals you've worked very hard for—so make sure you're also setting some goals for how you want to live in the next year, the next five years, the next ten.

2. Let go of outcomes we can't control.

When I wrote my first book, I hoped that in some small way it would help people make decisions about money that were more aligned with their values. My goal wasn't to write a *New York Times* bestseller but instead to help people. Even though I started out with the right intention, I sometimes forgot that goal and instead focused on the things that were outside of my control, like sales and reviews. And, no surprise, it led to anxiety and often disappointment. Whenever

I found myself spiraling into worry about the things I couldn't control, I tried to get back to the things I could.

Similarly, we can't control what the stock market does day to day, or even year to year, but by focusing instead on how much we spend and how much we save, we can get our focus back where it belongs.

3. Let go of worry.

I know how hard it is to stop worrying about money. After all, many of the things we worry about have a financial component. What if my retirement account dries up? What if I can't afford to send my kids to college? Worrying is a hard habit to break, but it doesn't do us any good. Can you think of one single thing that got better because you worried about it?

Of course, as anyone who's ever been told "Stop worrying!" knows, it's easier said than done. Just what exactly should we do when we start worrying? A good starting place is to do our best to get back to the process of living our lives according to the values we identified in the beginning of the book. Not surprisingly, not one person I've worked with has ever identified "worry" as a value.

4. Let go of our need to measure ourselves
    against others.

Human beings are competitive. We compare ourselves with other people both out of a desire to "win" and sometimes just to assure ourselves that we're "on the right track." Whenever I feel my urges to compare and compete kick in, I remind myself that, at the most basic level, what's driving that behavior is a desire to be happy. Often, I can snap myself out of this competitive thinking by reminding myself that my values have nothing to do with my neighbors'. For me, happiness is spending time with my family and serving in my community, and that has very little to do with competing with my neighbor.

IS MINE BIGGER THAN YOURS?

How Badly Do You Want It?

A few months ago, I had a conversation with an acquaintance who, by all accounts, would be considered highly successful. He had a thriving business, he was a private pilot, and he took plenty of vacations—although they were always a little stressful. His life was "full gas" all the time—he was either working really hard or playing really hard.

He told me that he wanted to make big changes in his life, like cutting back on work, maybe even changing jobs completely. He swore up and down that he really wanted to do it.

When I asked him why it hadn't happened, he explained that he didn't have enough savings to make the change. "But you're making tons of money," I said.

"Well, yes," he said. "And I don't really want to give that up."

And now we identified the real problem. He didn't want to make the change badly enough to make the sacrifices required to get there.

When people tell me about a goal they have in mind and their struggles to reach it, it's usually an important goal, connected to their career, their families, or some sort of personal achievement. When they tell me about their problems achieving it, I ask them, "How badly do you want it?"

Their responses tend to fall into two categories:

1. I want it badly, and I'll do whatever it takes to get there.
2. I want it badly, but I don't think it's possible for me to do.

Think about those two answers for a minute.

If you answered that you'll do whatever it takes, you've made a choice. You've decided that this goal means enough to you that you'll pursue it until you achieve it. I don't worry too much about these people.

But if you answered the second way—that you don't think it's possible—then I have to wonder if you really want it. I typically follow up with a few more questions:

- *What have you tried to help you achieve the goal?*

- *What sacrifices have you made?*

Most of the time, this process helps people discover that they've written off their goals as impossible without even trying to achieve them.

We can all be guilty of giving up because a goal seems out of reach. Or perhaps we talk a lot about how important our goals are to us, but do little to actually achieve them. In either case, we should stop and ask ourselves, "How badly do we want it?"

Here's the thing about goals: the ones that matter often involve a sacrifice. It can be tough to break patterns and deny ourselves instant gratification in order to stay focused, but when the goals are important enough, it's always worth it.

What are you prepared to sacrifice in order to focus on some important goal? If you can't come up with anything, perhaps the goal wasn't as important as you thought. Hopefully, however, this question already has you evaluating how much you needed those new headphones or that pair of shoes.

By now, I'm sure that you have at least a couple of goals in mind, and a good first stab at your one-page plan. Make sure to give yourself permission to not obsess over them. Remember that they're guesses. When you feel your goals and priorities shifting, ask yourself whether it's time to break out the Sharpie once again.

GET REALLY CLEAR ABOUT
YOUR CURRENT LOCATION

NOT long ago, my friend Steve asked me to help him get his finances in order. Steve was about forty with two teenagers who'd begun looking at colleges. Suddenly the idea of retirement didn't seem like just a faraway dream. Things were starting to feel "real," and he just wanted to make sure he was doing the right thing.

After we discussed his values and goals, I asked him where he stood financially.

As it turned out, he wasn't exactly sure.

Now Steve's a corporate CFO—but despite his ability to manage the finances of a large organization, when it came to his own finances, things were a little fuzzier.

Steve was hardly alone: most people don't have a very clear understanding of their current financial location. Part of me is continually surprised by this. In many ways, assessing where you are today is one of the simplest aspects of financial planning. After all, you don't need to guess about the future, or think hard about what really matters. All you have to do is tally up your assets and liabilities.

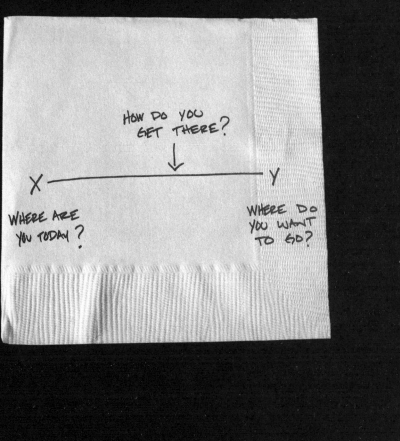

But the other part of me has been there—I know exactly what it's like when you just don't want to know.

Why is it so hard to take a clear look at our current financial state?

As soon as we start looking at our assets and liabilities, we're forced to deal with a lot of mistakes and missteps we may have spent months or years trying to forget. Even seemingly small liabilities can send us straight into avoidance mode. One friend told me about a doctor's bill that sat in her drawer for months until eventually she got a notice from a collection agency—all because she didn't want to think about how she'd failed to get it reimbursed by her insurance company in time.

Those small debts can add up, but the big ones can push us past our breaking point. I once met with a woman who had borrowed around $6,000 several decades earlier for a student loan. For years, it had been keeping her up at night, but she didn't want to face it. When she finally called the company that had issued the loan, she learned it had snowballed into a $34,000 debt.

This is the monster so many of us are hiding from: How on earth are we supposed to tackle something so huge? Is this debt going to breathe down my neck for the rest of my life? Can't we just pull up the covers until we have more money than we do now?

Once she was ready to deal with the debt, we were able

to put a plan in place that she's following today, but the fact that she'd been avoiding it for so long made it a lot harder than it needed to be.

The only way to get past this often painful moment and move on to what really matters is to do our best to put aside our emotions and focus on the facts. If you've made some missteps, do what you can to focus on moving forward. If your spouse blew your budget with some big-ticket item that hasn't been paid off, it's time to forgive, learn from the mistake, and deal with what's right in front of you.

This process is going to involve getting up close and personal with some of your baggage—but that doesn't mean you need to figure out a way to fix everything right now. We'll get to the matter of getting things back on track later in the book. For now, all you need to do is get clear about where you are. Without that clarity, you'll never be able to take the necessary steps toward meeting your goals.

About those goals: You have permission to forget about them for a moment. You're going to absolve yourself of any responsibility you feel to figure things out right now and simply get clear about where you are: by creating a personal balance sheet.

Things Just Might Not Be as Bad as You Think

My friend Steve had been putting off this process for a long time. But after I asked him to simply list his assets and liabilities—everything he owned and everything he owed— he realized he was in a lot better shape than he'd imagined.

"You know, we've been really aggressively paying down our mortgage," he said. "I hadn't really thought about it, but that's really made a big difference the last couple of years."

He also was reminded that they'd been systematically plugging money into their 401(k)s and the kids' savings accounts. Neither he nor his wife had really been obsessing about the accounts—they hadn't looked at either since they automated the process years earlier.

Steve quickly learned that their anxiety had been unfounded. Simply by doing some of the things every financial book will tell you to do, they were in a lot better shape than they realized.

Steve was hardly alone in this discovery. Many of my friends and clients have been pleasantly surprised that their assets are a lot more robust than they had imagined or their debts were not as bad as they thought.

Of course, for many of you, this process will be a different kind of reality check. I know it's going to be harder for you to pick up the phone and start calling creditors because I've spent more time adding items to the liability side of my balance sheet than I'd like to admit. When I realized I could no longer make my mortgage payments and I'd reached the end of my credit line, I couldn't bear to go through this process.

My anxiety about the situation affected my health. The pain would start in my stomach, and then I'd spend hours vomiting. It happened once, then three months later it happened again, then one month later it happened yet again. Eventually, it was happening every couple of weeks. The doctors couldn't find a physical cause.

I remember feeling like there was a small leak in the dam above our town, but no one wanted to face the fact that the dam's going to burst. Finally, it hit me: I had to be the one to do it. I remember thinking, Nothing's going to change unless I figure out where I am today.

When I finally sat down and said, "Okay, how bad is it?" I realized that not only was I going to lose my house, I would also have to lose the image of myself I'd been clinging to. I wasn't someone who always made smart financial decisions. As difficult as it was to get myself to face reality, as soon as I did, I was surprised to feel some sense of control returning. I can deal with this, I thought. It just might take some time to get there.

One of the first things I did was return my car. The lease on my Passat was up, and though I'd planned to get an Audi A6 at the same dealership, I knew we could no longer afford it. That didn't mean facing up to the reality was easy, exactly: I was friendly with the manager of the dealership and he knew my plans. I certainly didn't want to admit to him that I just couldn't afford the car—what would it say about me? I turned the key in and felt—*embarrassed* isn't the right word.

I remember it was gloomy that day. It was raining, which never happens in Las Vegas. I left the dealership with no car, which ushered in a period of three years where my family of six learned to make do with one car in a city where public transportation is nearly nonexistent.

It was hard, but also the right decision. As gloomy as that day was, I remember that I also experienced a flash of clarity. "This is reality," I thought, after I turned in the keys. "This is the right decision." When people would ask me what happened to the new car or ask me how my wife and I could live with just one car with a family of six, I would have to tell them we were cutting back. It wasn't the story I wanted to tell, but it was the truth. As you create your own balance sheet, remember that almost every line will tell a story—be prepared to question them.

If this all feels heavy to you, please take my word for it: The really difficult moments are only temporary. They will pass, and you'll be okay. Remember, ignoring the dam that is about to burst won't fix things. The sooner you start the work of repairing it, the better off you'll be.

Creating a Personal Balance Sheet

Once we get past all the drama and emotional resistance, creating a balance sheet is actually quite simple. All you're going to do is list what you own and what you owe. You don't need a fancy spreadsheet or even a computer for this exercise. Just grab a blank piece of paper and a pen. Then draw a line down the middle.

On the left side, list all your assets in detail. Bank accounts, the fair market value of your home, your investment portfolio. For every asset, list it and its value. On the right side, list all your liabilities. Credit card debt, mortgage, school loans. Again, get specific and list the actual amounts of each liability. (If you're wondering why I'm even taking the time to walk you through something so simple, it's because I keep crossing paths with people who've never done this.)

To help my friend Steve create his list of assets, I asked him questions like:

- *How much do you have in savings?*

- *What's the value of your house? (Don't worry about getting an appraisal. You can get a fair estimate using*

Zillow or factoring in what you know about the market and friends' houses.)

- *What do you have in investments or retirement accounts?*

After we created the list, I asked Steve, "Okay, now, what do you owe?" He began to list things like:

- *Credit card debt*

- *Mortgage balance (remember, you already listed the fair market value on the left side of your sheet)*

- *Other loans (car loans, student loans, etc.)*

If you're not sure about any of the numbers, call your bank, credit card company, or advisor. When it comes to debts, guessing isn't allowed, so take whatever steps you need to get the real numbers on the page. When it comes to assets, estimates are fine, but strive to be as accurate as you can.

Then add up all your assets and subtract all your liabilities. You now have your net worth.

Calculating Your "Emotional Balance Sheet"

The task of creating a balance sheet can become even more daunting when we bring in a spouse or family member—it's very difficult not to start playing the blame game when we have to dip into our savings to pay down a credit card bill someone maxed out.

My friend Beth recently discovered this when she and her husband, Chris, started having some conversations about money. Beth had paid most of the rent the previous year so that Chris could take on a bigger stake in his company; it meant a dip in his annual salary but seemed to make sense as a long-term investment. A few years earlier, he'd paid rent so that she could pursue a job opportunity that paid less but taught her a great deal about her profession.

As they talked about it, they realized both of them had been feeling like their "sacrifices" were a bit unappreciated. It was an "Aha!" moment for them both. Why were they still thinking about money as "yours" or "mine"? Sure, they each had individual goals, but what was most important to each of them was having flexibility to pursue projects that excited them. But resources were not unlimited. In order to help each other meet their goals, it would mean they'd need to take turns working longer hours.

The discussion helped remind them how aligned their goals were. Suddenly, they were talking about the shared dreams they hadn't discussed since the early days of their marriage—the places they wanted to travel and the impact they wanted to have on their industries.

The discussion ended up being one of the most important they'd ever had, but that doesn't mean it was easy for them to get to that place. Before they sat down and started talking about this, both felt like they'd been giving more than they'd been receiving. They'd been fighting about money without really knowing why.

When you're doing this work with a spouse or loved one, expect a lot of old resentment to bubble to the surface. My suggestion is to be completely honest about any "emotional assets and liabilities"—and don't limit yourself to thinking in terms of salaries and monetary investments. Remember the different kinds of human capital I introduced in chapter 1? Maybe one person hasn't brought in as much income as the other, but they've made other valuable investments: they put time and energy into taking care of the kids or running the household.

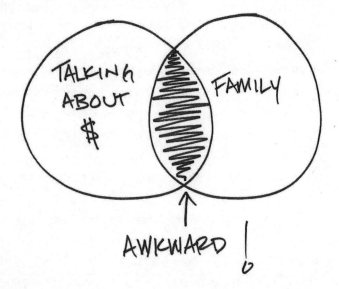

Keep as open a mind as possible, and do what you can to make peace with the past. Approach the process with empathy, and don't forget that the reason you're doing this probably has nothing to do with the material things we often fight about. Don't let your mistakes poison the opportunity to work together and move forward.

Drop the Blame

George Soros once tapped into something most of us know, but don't like to admit: "Once we realize that imperfect understanding is the human condition, there is no shame in being wrong, only failing to correct our mistakes."

We've got to stop beating ourselves up over financial mistakes. But we also need to take responsibility for what we've done. My experience losing my house has changed just about everything about how I do financial planning and the advice I give in public. For one thing, I am less quick to judge other people's financial behavior. I'm also more inclined to take into account personal factors that determine how people behave around money.

But despite all I've lost, the experience has been a surprisingly valuable one. I always knew the process would be tough, but I never knew how much clarity it would give me about how to move forward. In retrospect, it makes perfect sense: if we don't know where we are today, how can we get to where we want to be tomorrow?

Revisiting Your One-Page Plan

Creating a personal balance sheet may have given you some new insights about areas where you need to focus. Before you go further, it will make sense to revisit it and factor in any new goals. Remember, you can revise your plan over time. The one-page plan should simply include the three to five things that are really important right now:

- *The answer to the question "Why is money important to me?"*

- *Your best guesses at your financial goals*

- *Any debts that you'll need to pay down*

In the next section, we'll go deeper into strategies for spending and saving. Your one-page plan will be there anytime you're feeling bogged down in the details and need a reminder of the big picture.

PART TWO
Spending and Saving

NOW that you've set some financial goals and gained some clarity about your current location and used that knowledge to create a big-picture financial plan, it's time to narrow the gap between where you are now and where you want to be.

Whether you've discovered that you owe more than you thought or you've identified some ambitious goals, I imagine you're feeling a bit overwhelmed. How will you ever pay down your debt? Where will you find the extra money? Where do you go from here?

If you've gotten clear about your values, goals, and current reality, you might be thinking it's now time to start talking about investing your money. Hold on. Before we get there, we need to talk about something really important first. Because you could have the best investing strategy in the world, but if you don't have any money to invest, it won't help you. So we need to spend a little time figuring out where the money will come from.

This next section will give you some tools to help you take control of your spending and saving today.

4.

BUDGETING AS A TOOL FOR AWARENESS

IN the summer of 2014, Amazon released a phone called the Fire. One person who had the chance to use it early on was quoted in the *New York Times* as saying, "I am going to buy a whole lot more things with this technology than I ever have before." He was referring to the phone's feature that allows you to snap a picture of a product or pick up a song you hear playing in the background and be given immediate information about where to buy it.

The Fire—and the enthusiastic response to it—seemed to me a signpost of where we are as a society. It's hardly the only example of a product or service that makes it easy for us to buy without thinking. Take Apple's new iBeacon gadget, a Bluetooth device that will send shoppers suggestions on products and offers the moment they enter an Apple store. Or just consider the way companies use our search histories to continue advertising to us long after we first typed "surfboard sale" or "leather jacket" into our browser windows. Even if we've consciously made a decision that we didn't need something, the ads follow us for months—until eventually, we're too tired or bored to stay disciplined; with just one click, we're suddenly the new owner of that thing we'd been strong enough to say no to so many times before.

No doubt about it, modern consumer culture is full of traps that lure us into buying many things we don't truly need. But that's only half of the problem. Sure, marketing departments have a lot to answer for, but ultimately, we're the ones buying. At some point, we stopped being American citizens and started being, first and foremost, American consumers.

If we want to take control of our finances, we also have to take responsibility for the many unnecessary purchases we've made—and understand that nothing will change unless we change our behavior.

We All Like a Good Story

What is it that causes us to swipe our credit cards or press "Buy"? Lots of reasons, but often because we've told ourselves a story to justify the decision. Here's one that might sound familiar:

"Sure, there are cheaper cars on the market, but we've researched all the options, and the decision we made is based on cold, hard facts."

Or how about this one?

"The new iPad isn't a purchase, it's an investment."

While there might be some truth to either story, we all know the real reason we're buying whatever it is we're buying: we want it. And there's often another story we're conveniently forgetting: we can't afford it.

We often tell ourselves stories in retrospect. We decide what we want, often for emotional reasons, and then we go looking for evidence to support the decision. As we gather the evidence, we carefully omit anything that doesn't fit into the story that ends with a purchase.

Telling ourselves the stories we want to hear and ignoring the ones we don't can wreak havoc on our savings—so what do we do instead?

First, we can cut ourselves a little bit of slack. Our desire to justify the things we want and tell ourselves stories to make them fit is a natural part of being human. Furthermore, in many cases, shortcuts can be useful. Given the explosion of consumer choices we're presented with each day, we don't really have the time to consider every single option. If you did, you'd be driving back and forth between big-box stores all day long with Amazon open in one browser window on your smart phone and eBay in another. (P.S.: If this describes you, you really need to keep reading!)

To save ourselves the hassle of considering every available option, we decide what we want and then gather a few facts to prove to ourselves, our spouse, and our friends that we did the right thing. Maybe we run some numbers on our new "investment"—or, more likely, we read about someone who ran the numbers. Then, if the narrative matches, we use that as evidence that we're doing the right thing.

It seems easy. A simple case of addition or subtraction.

Things get complicated pretty quickly, however, when we start using the argument of saving money as a Trojan horse to hide the real reasons we're doing something. For example, take hybrid cars. Say you wanted to buy a hybrid or electric car. It's pretty easy to find evidence to support that decision, especially if you identified "I want to make a positive contribution to the environment" as a core value. But be careful if you're justifying the decision by saying it will save you money.

With few exceptions, the added cost of the fuel-efficient technologies is so high that it would take the average driver many years—in some cases, more than a decade—to save more money than they would with a comparable new model with a conventional engine. Gas would have to approach $8

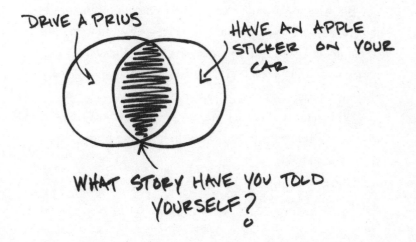

a gallon before many of the cars could be expected to pay off in the six years the average person owns a car.

To be clear, there are plenty of legitimate reasons to buy a more fuel-efficient car. Unfortunately, with a few exceptions, saving money isn't one of them. Which raises the question: why do we feel like we need to attribute every decision to the amount of money it will save us?

There are plenty of reasons: Because our society places a lot of value on the cost of things. Because we often don't want to admit we really want something. And because it looks good on paper . . . although, in many instances, if you look a little closer, you get a different story.

As another example, I read articles all the time that insist you should buy a house if you are currently renting. The articles typically provide a list of reasons why it would appear that buying will save us money. This is a classic case of using tons of "evidence" to tell a nice little story while ignoring the data that might not fit nicely in the narrative.

But we know it's not that simple. What if housing prices fall 10 percent and you have to relocate for another job? What about real estate commissions, closing costs, maintenance fees, and taxes? With a little research and honesty, there goes that nice, clean "time to buy" story.

While cars and houses might require the most complex stories, we spin tales about everything from vacation deals to buying in bulk.

Our goal for this chapter is to replace those stories with a much better one—the truth.

Tracking for Awareness

What if I told you there was a way to separate the stories we tell ourselves from the truth? And that there's a way to use that knowledge to make better decisions going forward?

Well, the good news is: there is. The bad news is: you've probably already heard of it.

It's called budgeting.

I know what you're thinking. There aren't too many people who love to track their spending. There aren't too many people who even want to think about it. Even if you don't mind budgeting, your spouse may hate it, or you may never have made a habit out of it as a couple—and so you find yourself doing it less and less and eventually not at all.

Budgeting clearly has a marketing problem. It's a bit like flossing. We understand how important it is to floss, but it's not something we like to even think about, let alone actually do. So we lie to the dentist about how often we do it and promise to do better, only to skip it again the next day.

Budgeting and flossing: both insanely important, super simple and, for many of us, nonstarters. But there's a reason for that. Many of us view budgeting as a punishment: a way to hold ourselves back from buying the things we want, a way to feel guilty about paying for the things we need. For many years, I avoided budgeting, viewing it as a task for people who aren't disciplined or who are overly obsessed with money. For me, sticking to a budget felt like being grounded. But I was wrong.

I talked about my reservations about budgeting with

Jesse Mecham, the founder of You Need a Budget, an online budgeting tool, and he shared an idea that immediately resonated with me: Budgeting isn't just about numbers. It's about awareness. In fact, budgeting equals awareness. Its purpose isn't to punish ourselves for spending money; it's to become very aware of how we're spending our money so that we have enough for the things that matter most.

BUDGETING = AWARENESS*

(*AND WHO DOESN'T WANT THAT)

I think anyone who takes the time to think about it would agree that spending money in a way that's aligned with what we value will bring us more happiness. So why aren't we doing it?

1. We don't think it's fun.
Budgeting requires being disciplined by setting and tracking spending goals. But being disciplined is hard, and people tend to avoid hard things.

2. We think we know where our money is going.
No, you don't. Sorry. Unless you track your spending, you don't know where your money goes. Nearly everyone I've seen go through the process of tracking for even just a month

has said some version of the following sentence: "I had no idea I was spending that much on *X*." Trust me, tracking will teach you something you did not know about yourself.

3. We're not sure we want to know.

You may be putting off budgeting because you know you've made some questionable decisions that you'd rather not examine too closely. Why did we buy that new television instead of contributing to our children's college fund? Why did we take the trip to Spain when we knew it would take months to pay off the credit card bills?

When we set a budget we have to ask questions like that. Then we have to decide: do we want to change our behavior?

Financial goals get funded with dollars—lots of them added up over time—and dollars tend to slip through our hands unless we have a system for plugging the holes. But you can't plug holes if you don't know they exist. That's where budgeting comes in.

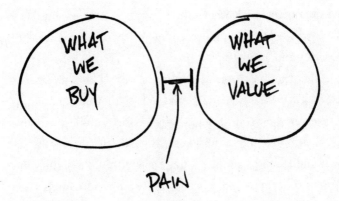

Not long ago I was having a discussion with my friend Dallas Hartwig, who cowrote the *New York Times* bestseller *It Starts with Food* with his wife, Melissa. He told me that one of their most important goals was to have the experience of buying property and building their own home. "But we'd need to save a lot more money," said Dallas, and they didn't know how.

"Why don't you track your spending?" I asked.

"I think it's because we're afraid of what we'll find out," they said.

Many people share this fear. But when they push past it, what they discover usually surprises them. One way to get over our fear is to ask ourselves if we're at least a little curious about where all the money goes. This curiosity inspired the Hartwigs to track one area in particular: the amount of money they spent on food. Food was, after all, a huge part of their life.

I asked Dallas if they were surprised at what they found.

"Surprised? We were horrified!" he said. They knew how important food was to their lives and careers, but they had no idea what a huge percentage of their income went to groceries and eating out.

After they got over the initial shock of this discovery, they had a few big realizations. When they began asking themselves these questions, they thought building a house was their most important goal. But when they really sat down and thought about it, they realized the flexibility and freedom they enjoy today was actually a lot more important.

By keeping their cost of living low, they can pack up any-time and work from another city. The reality was: owning a house was just a goal everyone told them would be impor-tant, but it wasn't what they wanted right now.

They also realized that their hefty food budget reflected the high value they placed on food. Their lives and careers center around the importance of our relationship with food—it was only natural that meals and groceries should play such a big part in their budget. In other words, their spend-ing habits and values were in alignment. They wouldn't change a thing.

A standard rule of thumb such as "Spend 4.5 percent of your income on groceries" would never work for the Hartwigs—as people who write a lot about food, it's too central to their lives for such a one-size-fits-all allocation. I told Dallas that their relationship to food sounded a lot like how my family views recreation. Whenever we track our spending, my wife and I can't believe we spent that much on time outside. But when we ask "What would we have taken out?" we realize that our trips are the very reason we work so hard.

Budgeting is important not only because it reminds us not to spend so much on gasoline or takeout, but also because it helps us cultivate the awareness we need to save and spend in accordance with our values. Budgeting forces us to face the reality of how we spend. It allows us the opportunity to see the gap between what we say is important to us and how we spend our money.

Where Do I Begin?

You can start by making a list of your fixed monthly expenses. Here are some common monthly expenses to think about as you get started:

- *Rent or mortgage payment*

- *Student loans*

- *Car payment*

- *Your minimum payments on any credit card debt you may have*

- *Utilities, insurance, cable, cell phones, etc.*

Remember to list any consistent expenses: prescription costs, therapist costs and other copays, gym memberships, etc.

If there are fixed expenses required for you to pay each month (what are often referred to as nondiscretionary expenses), automate your payments. I also recommend automating any long-term savings goals you've decided upon. Don't just say you want to save $500 a month; do something about it. As with your fixed expenses, you can automatically transfer a set amount to savings or investment accounts every month. Don't force yourself to make the decision to save every single month. (If you do, I guarantee you'll frequently find an excuse not to make the transfer.)

Now you're ready to start reviewing your discretionary

spending. I strongly encourage people to do so once a week, at least in the beginning. Again, we're aiming for awareness, not judgment. You "think" you only spend so much on coffee or eating out, but what do the receipts show? When budgeting, you need to make sure the perceived numbers match the real ones.

Throughout this process, you may become aware that you're paying too much for utilities or other services. For instance, before you flip the switch on automating your mortgage, make sure you understand the payment breakdown. If you're still paying for insurance you no longer need, contact your bank and take the necessary steps to drop the insurance. If you determine that dropping some monthly expense—subscription to a music site, premium cable—will help you reach your goals faster, don't wait to make the change. Automation is about simplifying your monthly finances, not checking out of the process completely.

Once you've got a good sense of your fixed expenses, start tracking:

1. Track everything you spend. You're going to track every penny you spend for a set period of time—it doesn't matter how small the cost. Maybe you'll be tempted to leave off the couple of bucks you spend on a bottle of water, but that's exactly the kind of expense that adds up and that we want to become aware of.

2. Use whatever tools will help you stick to the process. It doesn't matter what tools you use; what matters is that this becomes a daily practice. There are sites like Mint.com that can help you organize and categorize your expenses. Some people carry around a three-by-five index card or download budgeting software. I like a budgeting program from the good folks at YouNeedaBudget.com. The reason why is because it places such an emphasis on manual entry. I personally think nothing beats manual entry—remember, our main goal for budgeting is awareness, and nothing makes me more aware of exactly how much I'm spending than writing or typing in those numbers.

3. Try to look at budgeting as empowering—and maybe even a little fun. Once I get into the swing of budgeting, I notice that it becomes easier to stick to it. I find myself trying to spend as little as possible so I don't need to enter in so many numbers—budgeting is one instance where we can use our competitive instincts (I want to keep my expenses as low as possible) and even our laziness (I don't want to bother typing in more stuff!) to our advantage.

4. Watch out for one-time events. When we're building a budget, there's no way to predict one-time financial events, like the car breaking down or the furnace going on the fritz. We should set aside some money each month to help cushion ourselves against these financial shocks.

CHANCE YOU'RE ABOUT TO DO SOMETHING STUPID
SAYING OUT LOUD "JUST THIS ONCE..."

But given the inevitability of these bumps in the road, why do we get sucked into other, supposedly "one-time" events that are totally within our control? I'm talking about one-time events that promise a big deal: think the Friday after Thanksgiving or Cyber Monday. It's one thing to set aside a holiday budget that you've planned and saved for; it's another to use "one-time events" like sales or promotions as an excuse to throw planning out the window.

Then there are the days when we tell ourselves we need a special treat, a pick-me-up to make a bad day better. It's not a big deal, we tell ourselves; it's just this once, and we've been so good that it won't make a big difference to our budgets. But what about the next time, and the time after that one?

I'm not saying that we should never do something special that requires some financial maneuvering. But we need to be honest about why we're doing it and the consequences that may follow. And if the spending happens often enough, we have to stop referring to these things as one-time events. Instead, we need to start accounting for them in our budgets.

But remember: if we continue to allow these optional, one-time events to, in fact, be regular, they can be the very things that stop us from achieving our dreams and goals. And the last thing we want to do is look back and wonder if that trinket was really such a good deal after all.

How Long Do I Have to Do This?

Many people who balked at the idea of budgeting end up embracing it as a daily practice. Others pick a month per quarter whenever they feel it's time for a recalibration. What's most important is that you use what you've tracked to determine whether or not your values are in sync with your behaviors.

Once you've tracked for a month or two, you'll have some solid information about whether or not you need to start rethinking any of your behaviors. This exercise can end up with a couple of different outcomes. Some people realize that they've been spending way too much on things that aren't important; they immediately pinpoint some changes they can make to take them closer to their goals. Other budgets help people see that things like organic food, travel, or continuing education are a lot more important to them than they thought: they've used this information to rethink their values and goals, making sure to factor in time and money for their new discoveries.

A Spending Cleanse Is a Great Way to Get Back on Track

I won't lie: Sometimes this process forces you to recognize that you may need to make some big changes. Tracking your spending may reveal some bad habits that you've managed to ignore or overlook. And sometimes breaking these habits takes radical action. It's not enough to have a few conversations with a spouse, a personal coach, or a shrink. Some habits require a complete intervention.

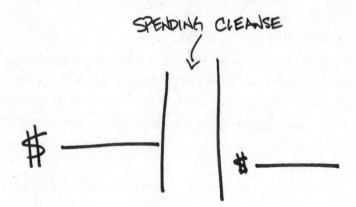

When I asked my friend Steve Fellows how he keeps his spending habits in check, he walked me through something he and his wife refer to as a "spending cleanse."

Every once in a while for several days, sometimes as long as two or three weeks, they do what they can to avoid spending any money. Steve rides his bike to work, they avoid eating out (including lunches), and they pass on any travel or movies.

This is hard, but this approach can help you cut out the nonessentials and get crystal clear about how you really want to spend your money and time. It may seem extreme, but it can shock you out of a rut you may have been in without even knowing it.

What about food? Go out Saturday and shop for a week in advance.

What about bills? Plan to pay them a day or two before you start and the day after you end.

What about trips? Don't go on any.

What about entertainment? This one can be interesting. Instead of going to the movies, go for a walk. Read a book. Go fishing. Ride a bike. Have a conversation. Draw a picture. There are plenty of things to do that won't require money. You can decide how strict you want to be, but the point is to bring awareness to your spending by taking a little break from it.

Your goal is to prepare yourself to go for several days, even longer if you can manage it, without spending a dime. I have managed to do it for a few days previously, and yes, it's hard, but it will be worth it.

It will be worth it to see where you're spending money out of habit.

It will be worth it to see if this changes how you think about money.

It will be worth it to see if it can stop some of your worst money habits, perhaps ones you only just discovered.

Most of all, it's a personal financial challenge that ultimately doesn't cost you anything but can pay huge dividends.

Still not sold on the concept of budgeting?

Turn budgeting into a game.

As soon as many people see the connection between budgeting and awareness, something clicks and they need no further convincing. But if you find yourself resisting turning it into a habit, let me leave you with one final idea.

Find a way to turn budgeting into a game by seeing how

few transactions you can have. Don't even worry about how much particular items cost—the goal is simply to limit the number of transactions each day. I know it doesn't totally make sense, but I've found this little trick keeps me on track surprisingly well.

When I get on a roll and have gone a few days without purchasing anything, I feel challenged to keep it going as long as I can. I'll do whatever I can to avoid having to manually enter in another transaction or carry around a receipt. I'll think about having to go through my Amex statement at the end of the month and set a goal to keep it as short as I can.

When I tell people about this little game, some are skeptical. "But you could just spend a thousand bucks at a store, couldn't you?" Sure—but whenever I challenge myself to reduce the number of transactions, I inevitably end up spending less money overall because what ends up happening is that I cut out a lot of those little nonvital purchases that have a habit of adding up over time.

It reminds me of the research done by BJ Fogg, who runs Stanford's Persuasive Technology Lab and who developed a methodology called "Tiny Habits" to help people make radical long-term changes to their behavior by taking baby steps. The classic example of Fogg's method is to develop a flossing habit by starting with one tooth at a time— or starting a running regime not with a mile, but with a block.

This may sound silly, but think about it: who's really going to floss one tooth? By setting the small intention, you end up going above and beyond what you set out to do before you know it. I've witnessed firsthand that this technique works with money. Start by aiming to reduce the number of transactions, and before you know it, you'll find yourself spending less money.

SAVE AS MUCH AS YOU REASONABLY CAN

WE'VE all heard the golden rule advising us to put away 15 percent of each paycheck for retirement. That sounds easy enough, right? The specific number makes things seem pretty black-and-white and the math seems to work out. If rules of thumb like this inspire you to start putting money away, that's great. In fact, many of my clients began saving in their twenties because a financial book told them to, and they're in much better shape a decade or two later than if they'd done nothing.

Unfortunately, there are a couple of problems with this one-size-fits-all advice: (1) you may not be able to put away 15 percent, or (2) you may not need to. What if you've gone through a spending cleanse and slashed your budget—and still, you find that you can't put more than 5 percent of your paycheck into savings? Or what if you just had a windfall year and made twice what you normally do? Are you just supposed to blow the extra money on stuff you don't need?

My concern about rules of thumb like this is that we often take them as absolute truths. When we do, they can put undue stress on those of us who are doing our best, yet still can't hit that 15 percent mark. I also have problems with any rules built around the assumption that we should work as much as we can now so that we can live comfortably when we retire. Life isn't just about retirement. And creating a financial plan should not be about putting such a rigid framework around your life that you deny yourself the things that help keep you healthy, happy, and sane today.

The process of making financial decisions is about more than building a spreadsheet, because life rarely fits cleanly into a spreadsheet. Many sound decisions can appear irrational if we don't know the whole story. Your aim should be to build a plan with the whole story in mind. By now, you've done a lot of foundational work to help you understand where you are and where you want to be; now you're going to use what you've learned to come up with a savings plan that makes sense for you.

How Do You Know If You're Saving Enough?

When I worked at Fidelity, I had a conversation with my friend Brad Petersen that changed my thinking about savings. Brad was also married with a kid, and he and I often discussed some of the issues that you have to deal with as a parent. One day, I asked Brad, "Are you saving enough for college, and how do you know?"

Brad's answer took me by surprise: "Carl, how about this: I'm saving as much as I reasonably can." It's been more than ten years since Brad answered my question, and I'm still thinking about his answer and what it means for the rest of us.

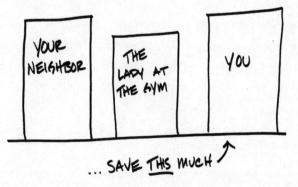

Of course, his answer presents us with a question: "How much is reasonable?" The answer is: "It depends." We all have different definitions of what "reasonable" means, but you're now armed with a bunch of information that will help you figure out what "reasonable" means to you. You've spent time creating your one-page plan. You now know where the money goes—and the emotions responsible for sending it there. It means you're perfectly positioned to get your arms around what "reasonable" looks like to you. Of course, there's a psychological hurdle we need to be aware of before we can come up with a plan.

Dealing with Instant Gratification

Without question, one of the biggest issues that stops us from saving is our need for instant gratification. Why save for something in the far-off future when we can buy something today? While I'm not letting you off the hook completely, there are some reasons why this issue trips many of us up.

It turns out that many people are horrible at connecting with their future selves. In a *New York Times* article, Alina Tugend highlighted some surprising research surrounding the way we view our future selves. Here, Tugend quotes Stanford health psychologist and lecturer Kelly McGonigal:

FUTURE FINANCIAL NEEDS

PERCEPTION

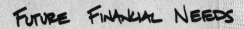

REALITY

"Brain scans, [McGonigal] said, have shown that there are regions of the brain that activate when we think about other people, and other regions that activate when we think about ourselves. In cases where people don't feel much connection to their future selves, the areas of the brain that light up when they are asked to think about themselves in the future are—guess what?—the same ones as when they think about other people."[1]

This tendency can make it challenging for many of us to adopt a reasonable savings strategy. Because we're so bad at seeing the future and fully recognizing the consequences of our decisions, it's easy to get sidetracked. On Monday, it may seem really reasonable to save an extra $100 a week, but by Friday, you're ready to treat yourself to dinner and drinks, bringing your weekly savings down to $25.

In the grand scheme of things, $75 in one week isn't a huge deal, but add that up over the course of one year, and it's almost $4,000. Now, even if you realize that's a number that can hurt over time, you might not be persuaded to sacrifice your happiness for your future self. Why let him or her ruin *your* life?

If so many of us are so horrible at connecting emotionally with our future selves, how do we define what's "reasonable"? We start with what we do know: where we are today and the awareness that came from budgeting.

Finding Money to Save

We've all heard traditional savings advice like ditching your daily coffee, packing a lunch, or taking public transportation whenever possible. It's good advice, especially if you need to make some drastic changes fast, but I suggest starting somewhere more personal.

Let's look at what you learned from tracking your spending. I bet a lot of what you discovered didn't surprise you all that much—you had probably anticipated that you'd see a fair slice of your paycheck go to things like coffee, gas, or eating out.

But that's not what I want to focus on: instead, I suggest you ask yourself which expenses weren't part of your regular routine, the ones that came as something of a surprise.

More often than not, it's the surprises that cause the heartburn. Maybe it was an unexpected trip to the bike shop, that lunch break you spent shopping online, the perfume you bought on a whim at the airport. In each instance, you didn't go looking for anything specific, but you ended up buying something anyway.

To be clear, I'm not talking about the major life events we can never anticipate—an illness, a car wreck, or a flooded basement. I'm talking about the surprises we had a *choice* in making. Fateful surprises are, thankfully, often once-in-a-lifetime events, but "surprise choices" happen time and time again. We have complete control over these "surprises"—and becoming aware of them is one of the best ways to change our behavior and start saving.

I used to really struggle with impulse book buying on Amazon. One day it hit me that I had piles of books I really wanted to read stacked everywhere—I had no idea when I'd have time to read all of them, yet I was still buying more books. That's when I implemented the 72-Hour Test.

Now, instead of buying immediately, I keep items in my shopping cart for 72 hours before I hit the checkout button. I was amazed at how quickly this changed my habit. Most of the time, the stuff sits in my cart for a lot longer than 72 hours, and I forget about it altogether.

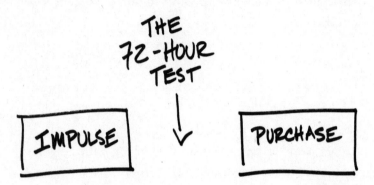

When I return to the site, I rarely feel as strongly about buying what's in my cart. So I delete those items, and in the process save myself a lot of money and the need to find more space. The nice thing about the 72-Hour Test is that very few things must be bought right *now*. The extra time provides a cushion: we're not saying "no"; we're simply not giving in to our urge for instant gratification.

You may discover even after applying these tests that you still need to be saving more. If that's the case, it may be time to kick your Starbucks habit or start taking the bus. But I strongly suggest you look at the surprise impulse purchases first. This process is not about denying yourself pleasure; it's about separating what's important from what isn't.

Don't Wait, Start Now

You've probably heard more than once that's it's important to start saving early. That you should start saving whatever you can when you're in your twenties to take advantage of the power of compound interest.

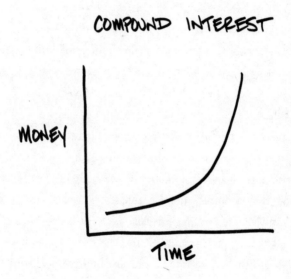

But what if you were too busy trying to pay a student loan and other bills in your twenties or, like many of us, had to use all the savings you built up to get through the last few years? Now with your savings a lot smaller than you know they should be, you feel like you missed the boat.

I thought about this when I read about the recent study that found nearly half of Americans wouldn't be able to come up with $2,000 in thirty days if they needed it. This reality hits home every time I have a conversation with people thirty-five and older who feel so far behind the savings game that they aren't sure what to do.

If you didn't start early, start now. Don't worry about what you did or didn't do already; just start. Your ability to move forward will be greatly improved if you don't spend too much time dwelling on the past. Yes, it's helpful to take a step back and look for patterns the way you did in chapter 4, but you need to approach it with a "no shame, no blame" attitude. Give yourself permission to use the past as a springboard to save more, not a billy club to hit yourself with.

When we get behind on our savings goals, we start to feel the pressure to make up for lost time. That pressure can often lead to spending hours looking for that home-run investment. It's a bit like a gambler doubling down to dig out of a hole. Stop hoping that a home-run investment will solve your savings problem. Maybe it's un-American to say this, but no matter how hard you work trying to find the next Apple, it's highly unlikely you will. Not impossible, just highly improbable. Stop waiting for the golden ticket; just start saving.

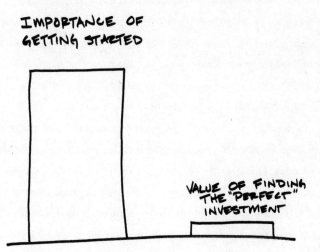

Whenever you start feeling the pressure to make up for lost time or come up with some clever investment scheme, take a moment to make sure you're not overthinking things. If you feel your mind start to spin, simply get back to the basics of saving:

1. Save as much as you reasonably can.
2. Spend less than you earn.
3. Don't lose money. You've worked really hard to get to the point where you've saved some money. Don't let the pressure of making up for lost time lead you to make speculative investment decisions. For now, just focus on saving and controlling spending.

Over time, you'll find ways to save more. You'll get better at avoiding impulse purchases or you'll decide it's worth it to cut back on other types of spending. For now, stop beating yourself up over what you didn't save in the past and start focusing on making today count.

Some Universal Tips for Saving

Let's be honest: what I think is reasonable and what you think is reasonable could be two different things. Two perfect examples are my clients Henry and Elizabeth, who decided to buy an RV so they could travel around the country with their kids. When we have dreams that are somewhat unconventional, often we want confirmation that what we're doing is reasonable. After looking at the numbers, I let them know that yes, they could afford it. Was it reasonable? For them, yes, because it was connected to the value they deemed most important.

Would it have been reasonable for Sara and Mark, the couple planning to take some time off to start a family, to plan such a trip? Perhaps not. At least not at that moment.

While we all have different ideas of what's reasonable, there are some savings techniques you may find helpful regardless of your goals and values:

1. Be more mindful of the money flowing in and out of your hands.

You've worked really hard at understanding how and why you spend money. Try to bring the same awareness to your savings. Yes, you may be hit with surprises that may mean putting away a little less this week, but whenever you feel the desire to dip into your savings, remind yourself *why* you're saving.

2. Save one-time windfalls.

Unless you're in the process of paying off a serious consumer debt, I strongly suggest putting tax refunds, inheritances, or money you receive as a gift right into savings. It will be incredibly tempting to treat yourself, but remember that you've already created a personalized plan that should be accounting for the things that are most important to you. One-time treats are rarely as important.

3. Automate savings.

I'm a big fan of automating certain financial decisions, and savings is probably number one on my list. If you've found $150 to save every month, set it up to transfer without any effort on your part. Taking the thinking out of the process will save you from debating whether you should spend that money or save it.

4. Set short-term goals.

There's no rule that says you can't save more one month than the next. Let's say you set your baseline of saving $150 extra, and automated the process. Now, that doesn't mean you can't save more in a given month. Don't shy away from setting a short-term goal of seeing if you can save even more some months. Maybe you can cut out your entertainment budget by spending more time outside in the summer months. Maybe you cooked a lot during the holidays and saved a lot of money you'd typically spend eating out. You can shift that extra money to savings without feeling any pressure to do the same thing the next month.

The Difference Between Need and Want

Now that we've discussed what's reasonable, it's worth addressing one aspect of saving that almost everyone will have to face. Don't be surprised if you end up with more goals than resources. Unless you have unlimited resources, you'll need to put a limit on your goals.

When we have to prioritize our goals, many of us become paralyzed, and as a result do nothing. Don't let the difficulty of the decision stop you from acting. As I've discussed, the only true mistake you can make when it comes to financial planning is doing nothing.

I think most people understand this reality on some level, but it's a discussion that doesn't come up very often when you're working on a traditional financial plan. The idea that we may not be able to accomplish all our financial goals doesn't square with the American belief that we can achieve whatever we set our mind to. I'm all for creating a financial plan that helps you meet your unique dreams and goals, but that doesn't mean I believe you can have everything you want.

Financial limitations can actually be something of a blessing in disguise. Over the years, I've discovered that figuring out what's most important about money can require taking a hard look at the difference between what we need and what we *think* we need. For many of us, this process will require a rethinking of our definition of "need." In a world where things we once considered luxuries have somehow become necessities, it can be difficult to separate needs from wants. Achieving clarity about the difference between the two may prove to be one of the biggest challenges—but also one of the most rewarding ones.

PART THREE
Investing

PEOPLE ask me all the time what I think about a particular stock or sector. They may have read an article about a new company, or fallen in love with a gadget that makes them certain investing in the company that made it is a sure bet. Whatever the reason, they're usually excited about some hot tip or hunch and they want to know, "Should I invest or not?"

I understand the desire to discover that once-in-a-lifetime stock that will erase all our financial worries. In fact, I'm right there with you. It may seem like a long time ago, but you probably remember a bit of the excitement in the nineties around tech stocks. I held out for a long time despite friends and family constantly telling me I was "missing out." One day I couldn't take it anymore, and I caved.

I bought $10,000 of InfoSpace stock—which was a lot of money then, and is a lot of money now. More money than I had to be investing in technology stocks. Despite the fact that I've advised many clients against buying a large chunk of stock in any one company, it felt good to join the ranks of tech investors. I was finally in on the secret.

As it turned out, the secret wasn't really a secret and I should have behaved for a little longer. Within months of my buying the stock, its value disappeared—along with my dreams of buying an island. Earlier this year, I got a reminder of my InfoSpace experience when the State of Utah contacted me about some unclaimed property. It turned out that my InfoSpace stock hadn't vanished completely.

I filled out the appropriate paperwork and waited anxiously for my check to arrive. I shouldn't have been surprised—and yet, part of me was—when I opened the envelope and saw that my $10,000 investment in InfoSpace was now worth about $81. I doubt I'll ever sell it because at this point, it's the perfect reminder of what can happen when I start to doubt everything I know about investing.

Now whenever people ask me for my advice about a particular stock or sector, I suggest they're asking the wrong question. Instead, I recommend they ask: "Does this investment fit into my plan?"

Questions like "Should I have gotten in on the Facebook IPO?" or "I use Apple products. Shouldn't I invest in their stock?" might seem to make sense when a company's stock hits a new high or a cool new product is released. But what happens when the stock falls, when a competitor arises, or when you trade in the product you loved so much just a year ago for another? Rather than making decisions based on short-term thinking and emotion, we want to make sustainable investment decisions. We want a plan in place that reflects our goals and values—and we want to stick to it.

When we commit to a plan, we're less likely to fall victim to our desires for instant gratification. We can feel confident that our plan is designed with our unique goals and values in mind; we realize maybe we don't need to hit the jackpot after all.

Of course, it's not just a desire to find a once-in-a-lifetime stock that derails us from a sound investment plan. It's also the way we think about investing that trips us up: When we hear the word "investing," our mind often jumps to the future. The point, we think, is to start making the right decisions today so that we can enjoy some payoff down the road. And that's, of course, a huge part of it.

But what if investing was *also* an opportunity to bring us peace of mind in the present? What if investing wasn't simply about setting your future self up for retirement, but also taking care of yourself—and your family—right now?

In this section of the book, we'll start thinking about investment a little differently. An investment plan shouldn't just be about where you put the money you have today; it's also about what needs to happen first. It's about identifying whether you need life insurance—and recognizing that you probably don't need very much to ensure that your loved ones are protected if tragedy strikes. It's about realizing that paying down debt can be the wisest investment strategy you'll ever make. And, most important, it's about separating real investment wisdom from the "carnival"—the massive financial entertainment industry built up around giving you information that not only isn't sound or helpful, but also has nothing to do with real investing.

Sure, it can be fun to imagine ourselves striking it rich by hitting on the right stock at the right time. But the odds that it'll happen are so small that I wouldn't plan on it. We don't know how the most recent IPOs will perform. We don't know how things will work out with the current crisis that's in the news. We don't know what will happen to the price of gold. But if we have a plan, we can know which kinds of investments fit into our long-term strategy.

BUY JUST ENOUGH
INSURANCE—TODAY

WHEN I ask my clients to tell me what's keeping them up at night, it usually doesn't take them long to respond. If they have children, or someone else who depends on them financially, they often tell me, "I worry about what will happen to my family if I'm gone."

If that's your answer to the question "What's keeping you up at night?" then the next step in creating your financial plan is clear: buy the right amount of insurance today.

For many people, life insurance is not necessary, but that's the point of this chapter: to help you figure out (a) if you need it, and (b) if so, how much you need.

Do You Need It or Not?

It's not unusual for people to put off the life insurance discussion. We come up with all sorts of reasons to avoid it. Often, we see it as important, but not particularly urgent, especially if our health is good. We figure we'll get to it later, once we pay down our credit card debt or after we've set up the kids' college plans.

But we also put it off because it's a decision that involves a very uncomfortable conversation. We have to translate a devastating emotional loss into financial terms. And we have to talk about what happens when we die.

I know this may be hard to accept, but for most of us life insurance plays one role: it replaces an economic loss. Insurance is an expense, not an investment. It's not a way to accomplish your investment goals or pay for an education. And perhaps most important of all, it can't replace an emotional loss. And so we're going to focus on buying just enough insurance

~~RETIREMENT PLAN~~   A WAY TO REPLACE AN ECONOMIC LOSS   ~~EDUCATION SAVINGS~~

for it to do its job, and the right kind of insurance—basic term life insurance—which, thankfully, is not that expensive.

For the purposes of this conversation, we're going to need to consider scenarios in which you or your spouse has died—it won't be easy, but it is essential to do our best to put aside the emotional dimensions of that loss and focus simply on the economic loss.

There's a simple rule of thumb to determine whether you need insurance:

If someone depends on you economically, you need life insurance.

But how do you define "dependence"? Let's look at a few scenarios to determine how to make that decision.

- *First, let's assume you're married, and you and your spouse have solid careers, but no kids. Would there be an economic loss if you passed away? Your initial instinct might be to say, "Yes," but you've got to be clear-eyed for a minute. While your income will be reduced and while that may be painful, you should have an honest discussion about whether you're able to deal with the economic loss—and if you can, then you don't have to worry about life insurance.*

- *In the second scenario, let's assume you still don't have kids, but you delayed your career or education to support your spouse's career. If he or she were to die, you'd be left with perhaps less experience, education, and income than you might have had otherwise. This qualifies as an economic loss, and life insurance makes sense in this situation.*

- *Now, consider a third example. In this situation, you have kids and all the financial goals that come along with them. You're going to have education to pay for, you're going to take vacations, and you're relying on both incomes to support those goals. In this case, if one of you were gone—in other words, if one of those incomes were no longer there—there would clearly be an economic loss. You'll need life insurance to close the gap between your plan and the reality.*

Even as I write this, I know how cold it sounds to determine whether the very real emotional loss of a spouse is also a true economic loss, but unlike some of the other financial decisions you'll be making, the decision whether or not to buy insurance is all about the numbers. Once we're able to get past the emotional component of the discussion, it's actually one of the easiest economic decisions to make. Let's walk through the steps, and, remember, your calculations don't need to be precise. We're going to take our best guess at the economic loss you'll need to replace.

Calculate the Economic Loss

Now that you've determined you need insurance, what do you do?

First of all, you need to calculate lost income—let me walk you through the process with an example.

Let's say you and your spouse are both working and you have children—and all the goals that go along with them. To make the math easy, let's say you each make $40,000 a year. Because you're relying on both incomes, you will need that $40,000 to replace that economic loss.

Of course, things aren't always that simple. Let's consider an example where just one spouse is working. If the non-working spouse passed away, it might seem like there would be no economic loss. But keep in mind that if one spouse were gone, the other would not be able to work as much: he or she might have to scale back hours at work and take on more household responsibilities that were shared or completely taken care of by a spouse working at home. (Of course, these are also considerations to keep in mind even if you're both working.)

But in the end, we need to come up with a number.

If your spouse made $40,000, you may need to scale back hours and lose a little of your own income—let's say $10,000.

That would mean you'd need to replace a total economic loss of $50,000 per year.

Start by calculating how much money you need to replace the loss.

To do that, you'll need to fast-forward a minute. Let's pretend you had an investment account, and the sole goal of that account was for you to be able to replace the lost income you calculated in step one—in this case, we calculated you would need to replace $50,000 per year.

While there's always going to be debate about how much you'll need, remember we're making guesses, so here's a rule of thumb: the 4 percent rule. Essentially, it means if your money is invested carefully in a diversified portfolio, you can feel comfortable taking about 4 percent each year (inflation is factored in) and not be too worried about running out of money over any thirty-year time period. Based on that, the next step is calculating how much you would need in that account.

Keeping the 4 percent rule in mind, the easy way to calculate how much you would need would be to take the annual amount (in this case, $50,000) and divide by 4 percent or .04.

In other words, in order to replace the $50,000 per year that you've identified, taking inflation into account, you would need a $1,250,000 policy.

Buy Term Insurance

"Term insurance" simply means you can lock in the cost over a specified period of time, and the cost won't change. You're essentially renting insurance; at the end of the period of time you've chosen, you don't have anything. Because of that, it costs very little compared with other kinds of insurance. Remember, it's not a savings or investment account. It's just doing its job of replacing an economic loss stemming from a death. You typically pay an annual premium to keep the cost in place and can cancel at any time.

Now you can determine the length of the term: ten, twenty, thirty years. You'll want to buy the longest policy you think you'll need based on your age because you're locking in the cost (and you may not be able to get the same rate years down the line if your health were to change). Twenty-year terms are pretty common. When considering how much you need, keep in mind factors like the age of your children—if your kids are almost out of the house, you may only need a ten-year term.

Because you can lock in the cost of the insurance and term insurance is so cheap, I suggest rounding up, because you can always cancel. If you win the lottery or sell your business, you're not locked into the contract; you just don't pay the premium.

Don't Let Fear Drive Your Decision

A few years ago, a salesperson came to my door and offered to sell me cancer insurance. I remember thinking, "Gosh, maybe I need that," and it wasn't long before I began to think about all the other kinds of insurance I might need—shouldn't I protect myself and my family against all the potential threats that might arise?

Ultimately, I decided against piling on all kinds of insurance "just in case."

Here's the thing about life. It's full of risks, and the decision to buy insurance boils down to deciding between the risks we're okay with and the ones we'd like someone else to take care of. Remember, your goal with life insurance is always to have as much as you need, but never more than what you need.

Who's Worth More?

When thinking about life insurance, you may end up having more discussions about your death than you ever anticipated. While they can be some of the most important conversations you've ever had, that doesn't make them easy.

Of course, it's not surprising that we avoid the discussion because it entails some discomfort. Who really wants to think about dying? About losing your spouse? About what will happen to those you love in your absence?

However, that's not the only point of tension that may arise. This topic will naturally lead to a question few couples or families want to explore: "Who's worth more?" One friend's parents dealt with this issue when buying insurance. Financially, the loss would be greater if her father died, but her mother was miffed that her husband had a bigger number on his policy.

I find myself in a similar situation. If I died, the economic loss would be greater than if my wife did. However, I know that my kids would be much worse off because my wife is the center of what makes everything work in our family.

Don't let the emotional aspect of this discussion derail you. Remember, it has nothing to do with the reason you're buying life insurance. Only by separating economic need from emotional loss can you determine which life insurance plan is right for you. Otherwise, you'll buy whatever the insurance salesperson is offering, and it may cost you in other areas of your financial life.

"THE BEST INVESTMENT I EVER MADE": BORROWING AND SPENDING WISELY

WHEN I was living in Las Vegas a client of mine named Chris was telling me about his investment decisions. "I've done everything right," he said. "I've saved my money and paid down my mortgage." It was true; his portfolio looked great and he was on track for retirement.

Then he added, "And I'm totally bummed."

Chris was upset because his business partner at the orthodontic clinic where he worked had taken the opposite approach. "He took out one of these aggressive interest-only mortgages," he explained. "Instead of paying down his debt, he invested heavily in more real estate and the stock market." To be sure, Chris's partner was heavily leveraged, but at the time of this conversation, Chris was disappointed because his partner's investments were valued at three times his own.

In my twenty years as a financial advisor, Chris was the only client I've ever had who actually complained about paying off his debt—but I suspect he's not complaining today. Why? Because our conversation happened in 2006—one year before the real estate market hit its peak. We all know what happened over the next couple of years—real estate got crushed, and most people who were heavily leveraged learned

WHEN IT COMES TO INVESTING...
THE ONLY GOAL THAT MATTERS IS YOURS

it's a double-edged sword. When you take that into account, his business partner's strategy doesn't seem so sound.

By now, you've got a clear understanding of your goals. You've probably had to make some tough decisions about your spending and saving. But you're probably wondering where debt fits into that discussion. For years, we've heard about the benefits of leverage and "good debt." You may have someone in your life like Chris's business partner who seems to be faring a lot better than you because he or she took on a lot of debt. You probably have plenty of debt-related questions: How much debt is too much? Which debts should you pay down first?

And, most important: is taking on debt ever a good investment?

To start with the answer to that last question: yes. There are definitely times in your life when borrowing can fit into your financial plan. In this chapter, I'll discuss how we can separate good, careful borrowing from thoughtless, "instant gratification" borrowing. I'll discuss the pros and considerable cons of taking on debt for various types of expenses and come up with rules of thumb for borrowing.

And I'll also introduce another way to think about debt as an investment strategy:

Getting rid of it can be one of the best investments you can make.

An Investment with a Guaranteed Return

Imagine if I offered you an investment opportunity that had a guaranteed return rate of 15, 18, or even 22 percent. I suspect that, even if money were a little tight, you'd find a way to get in on the ground floor.

And yet, if I told you that you could make the same amount of money by paying down your credit card debt, you'd probably find a number of excuses why that just isn't possible right now.

Just as with any kind of spending, we often justify borrowing by telling ourselves a story. Some stories make more sense than others, like taking out a mortgage after you've put 20 percent down. Others, well, they sound more like fairy tales. Drawing the line between the two will rely in large part on your goals and values. Using those two reference points, you'll have a way to figure out how to say "No" now so you can get to a much bigger and better "Yes" later.

For instance, if you can say "No" to borrowing money to buy an engagement ring (you do not need to spend three months' salary on a ring!), you're leaving room to say "Yes" to buying your dream home in a few years. If you say "No" to buying a new TV on credit when the old one still works, you increase the odds that you can say "Yes" when you need to replace your decade-old car.

To be clear: These won't feel like easy decisions. When you're in the moment, it may seem like all signs point to saying "Yes." That's why it's so important for you to be really clear about what's most important to you.

I also encourage you to keep challenging your definition of investment. We're used to thinking of investments as putting money aside today to increase our returns tomorrow. But when we're in debt, we need a more immediate investment goal: what if we widened our definition of investment to include smart decisions about systematically decreasing our debt?

At some point, you've probably heard the old saying "People who understand interest earn it. People who don't pay it." Borrowing carefully includes more than just knowing the best time to sign on the dotted line. It also means understanding how to deal with the debt once you have it.

The Most Basic Rule of Investing: Earn More, Spend Less

During the financial crisis, personal credit card debt took a dip. While we know the negative impact it had on our consumer-driven economy, on a personal level it at least meant that many of us were reining in our consumer debt. Unfortunately, in 2014, only six short years later, credit card debt is ticking back up.

While the U.S. government can increase its debt ceiling with a vote in Congress, we don't have that option in the real world. When we're about to max out our own credit cards, we have two choices:

1. Earn more
2. Spend less

It's simple math that requires tough choices. If you spend more than you earn, at some point you'll have to make some changes. While the "earn more/spend less" equation is simple, that doesn't mean it's easy. I know what it feels like to tell my kids that we simply can't afford to do something that was incredibly important to them. My wife and I have had the awkward discussions about which expenses needed to be cut to make ends meet. These conversations aren't easy, but they need to happen if we want to achieve the goals that are most important.

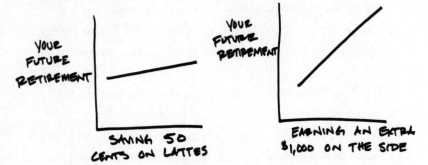

To add to the frustration, these decisions are intensely personal. We all want a magical formula that will propel us back into the black. But getting out of debt doesn't work that way. It usually comes back to what you're willing to sacrifice. But you can't know what you'll need to sacrifice until you understand all your debt.

Paying Down Debt Is an Investment

If you're holding on to debt with high interest rates, paying those debts down trumps just about any other financial investment you can make. Consider this: right now, if your investments are doing well, you might be earning around 7 percent.

Now look at your credit cards. Even if you're careful, you're probably paying more than 15 percent. Does that make any sense to you?

Remember, paying down debt is an investment with a guaranteed return. So figure out where you have the most to gain. Pick the debt with the highest interest rate and start throwing all the money you can at it. This idea, known as the "debt avalanche," isn't a new one, but it's very effective.

Once you've identified the debts with the highest interest rates, you can pick them off one at a time. When you're done with one, go to the next. While you're going through this process, I can't emphasize enough how important it is to avoid the trap of continuing to use your credit card. If you can't pay the balance off every month, you're preventing yourself from saying "Yes" to whatever it was you decided was most important to you.

Unfortunately, because credit card companies make it so easy to take on consumer debt, we treat it very casually. Don't. How you handle this debt matters even more than your investment rate of return because of credit cards' high interest rates. Keep that in mind the next time you're about to swipe a card for something you "need."

Should You Buy a House?

The biggest borrowing decision most people will ever make is whether or not to buy a house. If you ask some people, they'll tell you, "It's the best investment I ever made!" Whenever someone has told me this, I've sat down with them and said, "Let's calculate exactly what your return is."

The returns usually end up somewhere in the ballpark

of 3 percent—and it no longer surprises me why. That number lines up with the data that Nobel Prize winner Dr. Robert Shiller has been providing for years on how fast home prices have grown across the nation. Housing prices grow about in line with inflation, and the average home price increase over the last two hundred years has been close to 3 percent.

So why are people saying it was the best investment they ever made?

Sadly, because it was the *only* investment they ever owned for that long.

Of course, buying a house is a complex decision because it involves so many factors. There are pros and cons to both sides and—as someone who is still recovering from the loss of my house five years ago—I know it can be really difficult to assess which option makes the most sense for you.

For the last three years, my family and I have rented a home. Most of the time that feels fine. But last year I found myself in a state of temporary panic when I read a tweet from the financial journalist Felix Salmon quoting billionaire hedge fund manager John Paulson: "If you rent, buy. If you own, buy a second home."

When I read it, I immediately felt anxious. I recognized the feeling: it's the one you get when you think you have to act on something right away or you'll miss out. After all, if John Paulson, the guy who made "The Greatest Trade Ever," was saying I should rush out and buy a house, I'd better get on it!

After allowing myself to get all worked up about this, I

did what I've done several times before. I pulled out a piece of paper and a pencil and worked through the emotions and the numbers. In the end, I was reminded of something incredibly important:

John Paulson doesn't know me or my situation.

There is absolutely no reason I should be making decisions based on something he—or any other "expert" sharing his guess about the direction of the housing market—says.

Still, this "best investment I ever made" argument runs deep. Around the time I was running the numbers, two people expressed similar concerns. They were convinced that if they didn't buy a house now, they'd be priced out of the market—and maybe they will be. But I heard that "Either buy now or regret it later" argument a lot in 2005 and 2006.

Then came a third conversation. An acquaintance needed to downsize to a different home after her children moved out. But even though selling and moving to a smaller home is the right decision (given her particular situation), she's holding off because the financial news and forecasters have been implying that the house could be worth substantially more sometime in the next twelve months.

This is madness!

Again, buying a home is one of the biggest financial decisions that most of us will make in our lifetimes. And yet it's often a decision in which the person with the most knowledge about the right course of action gets overlooked: you.

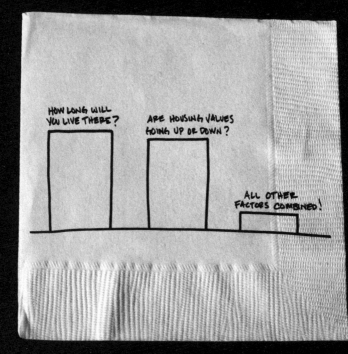

There's a simple way to fix this problem. All it takes is a piece of paper, a pencil, and some time. If you're struggling with this decision to buy (or sell), take a minute to think through these questions and write down the answers, because I suspect you'll need to refer back to them the next time somebody decides to share what he thinks will happen with the housing market. This list is not meant to be prescriptive. It is meant to get you thinking about something other than forecasts and guesses.

Ask yourself the following questions:

1. Can you afford it, and do you have enough saved for a down payment? Make sure you include the cost of things like property taxes, homeowner association fees, and utilities.
2. Can you qualify for a loan? If the answer right now is no, then you can stop torturing yourself, because it doesn't matter if the market is about to take off. You can't buy a house.
3. How long do you plan to live in the home? There's some debate about the minimum time you should live in a home for it to be worthwhile, but if it's less than five years, forget about it. If it's five to ten years, you can consider it seriously, and if it's ten or more years, the numbers will likely fall in your favor.
4. What guess are you making about housing prices? It is a painful reality that the one variable that makes a huge difference in this decision is unknowable. What is going to happen to housing prices in the short term is anyone's guess. But for your own sanity, just assume that housing

prices will continue to increase by about the long-term average of inflation, or 3 percent per year. You can't afford to buy a house if the decision depends solely on what you think the house might be worth some day.

Remember, the answers to all of these questions will depend on your situation. And that's the point. Hopefully, it's clear now how ridiculous it is to buy a house just because some expert who knows nothing about your situation told you to.

You may discover that buying and owning a house isn't for you, and that's okay. Despite what many people believe, renting is not "throwing money down the drain." Nor will it prohibit you from buying at a later date.

Take my friend Rick, who needed to move to a new city for his job. Because he didn't know how long he'd be in this particular location, his family rented rather than bought. Every month Rick hated writing that rent check—until he started to notice how much he was saving. Because he didn't have any property taxes or maintenance fees to deal with, Rick was able to put a lot of money into what he called his "house account." After a few years, he'd managed to save a nice chunk of money that came in handy when it was time to relocate again—this time to a town where it made more sense to buy.

Compare that with my situation. I owned a home during the same time period that was putting me deeper into debt. So out of the two of us, Rick was clearly better off.

Don't assume that you *must* own a home. And never buy a house solely because of the tax benefits. Borrowing a dollar to get sixty cents back in the form of a mortgage tax credit will only lead to disappointment—especially if it means you'll have to sacrifice some of the goals you've identified as the most important.

Should I Be Paying Down My Mortgage?

Whenever anyone asks me about mortgage debt, I walk them through the following exercise.

Take out a piece of paper.

1. One the left side of the paper, draw a circle: inside, place your mortgage interest rate (which you should have identified when creating your personal balance sheet). Say you have a 5 percent mortgage interest rate: write 5% in the circle. (You may be able to factor in a small mortgage rate deduction—but keep in mind the rate will vary depending on where you live and other factors.)

2. On the right side of the paper, draw a square, and in the square, write 8% with a big question mark. This number represents your best guess at how your investments will do.

Here are two investments: One's going to earn you a 5 percent guaranteed return. One gives you a shot at an 8 to 10 percent return. Which one would you pick?

Here's what many financial experts will tell you: why would you ever pay off your mortgage rate at 5 percent or lower after taxes when you could use that extra money instead and invest it at 8 percent?

On a spreadsheet, this argument looks great. But here's

what the spreadsheet doesn't take into account: the *question mark*. An 8 percent return sounds great, but there's simply no certainty it will ever come to fruition.

Here's what I want to emphasize about this exercise. One investment is guaranteed. That's your mortgage. The other has historically given you an 8 to 10 percent return, but there's no guarantee associated with it.

In the final chapter of the book, I'm going to talk a lot about behaving when it comes to our investments: sticking to our plan even when financial experts and the media are calling for us to abandon ship and follow whatever new trend people are shouting about. I mention this now because I've found it's very difficult for people to behave with "house money"—money you've mentally accounted for even if there's no guarantee that your house will be worth what you think it will in ten or twenty years.

Experts who ignore the question mark will tell you to invest the money that you could be using to pay down your mortgage in the stock market for twenty years—the idea being that at the end of twenty years, you'll be able to pay down your mortgage ten years earlier.

It's a beautiful idea and it works perfectly on a spreadsheet. But here's the thing. I actually can't think of anyone who's done this successfully. I'm sure they exist, but in my close to twenty years in this business, I've never actually seen anyone who bet on the question mark who is really happy with their results.

I have, on the other hand, met a lot of people who've felt the elation that comes from paying down their mortgages. I've attended mortgage-burning parties. And I can think of only one person who complained about paying down his mortgage rather than investing the money—and his complaint came right before the housing meltdown.

Even though it may not make sense on a spreadsheet, even though I can *build* you a spreadsheet that says it's not a good idea, every client I know who's gotten debt-free or stayed debt-free has felt good about it.

Sometimes It Pays to Spend a Little More

Given my warnings about the dangers of debt, what I have to say next may surprise you: when it comes to borrowing (or any kind of spending), sometimes it pays to spend more.

Do you buy the more expensive option or do you always go with the lowest price? As with most things, the answer will depend in large part on what you've said you value most.

Take a friend of mine who never understood why his neighbors would take on debt to pay for things he didn't care about, like big houses and expensive cars. To him, these things simply weren't worth the money. When, one day, he was being particularly grumpy about it, I asked him about his family's spending habits.

I had noticed that compared with most families I knew, his family appeared to spend a lot of money on vacations and even more on recreational gear. My friend's a smart guy, so it took only a moment for him to see the disconnect. Both my friend and his neighbors spent money on things and experiences that they really valued—but, of course, their values were different.

It's not unusual to spend more money on the things that really matter to us. We probably all have areas where a cheaper substitute won't cut it. However, when we spend more without first building a framework for making these decisions, it's the kind of behavior that can blow up budgets and lead us to spend more on things that aren't worth the extra money.

Spending a lot of money on something—even something

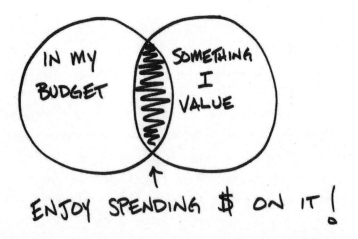

you'd consider a luxury—doesn't necessarily mean you're making a bad financial decision. It may well be the best decision for you. But only if it's in line with your goals and values.

The more we can make money decisions that support our values—including when and how we borrow money—the less likely we'll regret those decisions, even if they're expensive choices.

Keep that thought in mind the next time you wonder if it's really worth it to spend more. Brace yourself: sometimes the answer will be "Yes," but you may need to say "No" to something else in order to afford it.

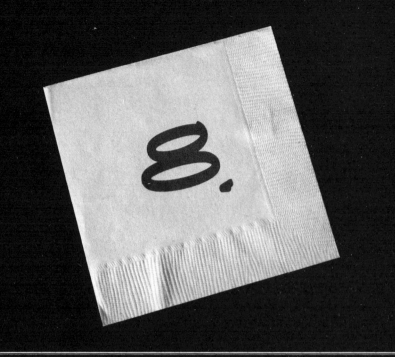

INVEST LIKE A SCIENTIST

AFTER decades of working with people to come up with unique financial plans, I've heard all kinds of goals and values. No two people have exactly the same answers to the question "Why is money important to you?" and no two portfolios ever look the same.

And yet there's one thing that many people share: a disillusionment with the stock market. I hear things like "It's just a giant scam" or "I lost all my money in stocks." Unfortunately, not too many people I talk to have been happy with their investment experiences.

I've thought about this a lot over the years, and concluded that this has a lot to do with how bombarded we are with opinions about how we *should* be investing. Every day, we're subjected to countless stories about people who have struck it rich and are told that if only we watch the right show or track the right indicators, we can join them.

The huge entertainment industry built up around so-called experts shouting frantic advice at us has left so many of us frustrated—and scared. And when we have followed their advice, too often it's left us with a fraction of what we put into the market and a lot of bad memories.

But here's the thing: if you look at the performance of the stock market over the last ten to fifteen years, you'll find it's actually done quite well.

What's the disconnect? Why have so many people told me that their attempts at investing have ended in failure even as the market as a whole is succeeding?

Because they're confusing *investing* with *speculation*.

SPECULATING   INVESTING

In fact, real investing has as little to do with CNBC programs as it does with Lifetime movies of the week. But we've been told we should know when to buy and when to sell. We've been told that's what investment is. When, in fact, speculating or trading and investing are completely different things.

I don't blame people for their confusion—I made the same mistake myself when I blew $10,000 on InfoSpace stock. At the time, however, it was easy to assume I was making the right choice.

Not only has the financial entertainment industry instilled the belief in us that we should all be watching the Dow like hawks, ready to swoop down when we see a stock we like and escape at any sign of trouble, but the financial services industry is built around these ideas, too. When I was a rookie trainee at Prudential Securities, one of my assignments was to go around and ask the more senior stockbrokers for tips. I remember that much of the advice was things like "You're only as good as your last trade" or "Have a hunch, buy a bunch."

Even those of us who can ignore the "carnival" can get trapped by the fallacy that our gut instincts based on our experiences or expertise can help us pick winning stocks. The idea that we can use what we know to make guesses about the stock market has been around for a while—but unfortunately, people don't realize that knowledge about a particular stock or company is just a starting place—and, even then, never a guarantee.

Take the way so many have misinterpreted the advice in Peter Lynch's classic book on investing from the 1990s, *Beating the Street*. The book helped walk readers through some of the research they should do before investing in a particular stock. But Lynch's more nuanced message was forgotten over time, and what many of us remember is the vastly oversimplified slogan "Buy what you know."

The "Buy what you know" idea is ubiquitous among individual investors. Many of my savvy friends in the media admit they've made bets about companies based on the quality of the films or TV shows these companies have produced. I've met with a real estate agent who assumed that because the Toll Brothers had just sold so many new houses in his community, the stock was about to catch fire. And I've had numerous conversations with doctors who believe they should buy stock in a particular drug company because they know there's been an uptick in prescriptions: surely that was a sign the stock was only going to rise.

In every instance, these are professionals who are hardworking, smart, and good at their jobs. They're informed enough to have some idea of what separates good companies from bad ones. Why wouldn't they be able to use that knowledge to make sound investment decisions? How hard can it really be?

Whenever people tell me they're thinking of buying Apple or Samsung stock because they love their new smart phones, I ask them, "Have you read their latest annual report?"

I don't even ask if they've read the quarterly report, visited the company, looked at what analysts have written about the company, or read interviews with the CEO. I simply want to know if they've read the last annual report.

No one has said yes.

Not because they're negligent or because they're not smart. Because they're *busy*. Much too busy to wade through hundreds of pages of financial statements. So they act on their gut alone—and a few months or years down the line find themselves making something I call the "Big Mistake": buying high and selling low.

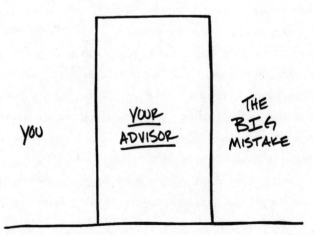

The belief that our gut instincts can help us predict the future of the market is the kind of magical thinking that can wreak havoc on your financial plan. It also has nothing to do with real investing.

Forget high-frequency trading, forget the charismatic personalities on CNBC, forget what your brother-in-law told you at your last barbecue. All of that is just distraction. If you want to keep watching because you think it's fun, that's fine, but you probably have better forms of entertainment.

When people tell me they've given up on the stock market, what they really mean is they're sick of the carnival. Which puts them in the perfect position to understand what investment really is.

The Science of Investing

A friend who also happens to be a doctor once told me that if he practiced medicine the way he'd been investing, he'd kill half the people he saw. When it came to his work, he would never prescribe a drug before reading peer-reviewed evidence to make sure all the trials went well—but when it came to investing, he assumed that he should be able to use his intuition to make good decisions. After all, he was smart and informed—how hard could it be to pick a few winners?

I suspect this reality applies to most if not all investors at some point in their lives.

But it doesn't have to. In fact, there's a better way.

I remember when I first started to learn about the science of investing. I was getting a professional designation taught by a professor at the University of Pennsylvania, and during one of the lectures, the professor introduced us to some of the work he'd been doing to help us approach investing in a rigorous, disciplined way. I remember thinking, "Where has this been my whole life?" It was like finding myself in a parallel universe.

Just as medical researchers have put their hunches to the test by beginning with a hypothesis, gathering data, doing blind testing, and getting their articles peer-reviewed and published in academic journals, so, too, have financial researchers been spending countless hours studying market performance. We don't hear much about the science of investing because it's, well, boring, but what they've discovered can be an excellent framework for building your unique investment portfolio.

A Framework for Investing

Part of the investor's dilemma is that no matter how much data we have about the past, we have no data about the future. No matter what history says about the long-term upward trend of the stock market, we still don't know for sure what the future will bring.

So after all the spreadsheets are put away, investing becomes a matter of faith. This act of faith is most evident when it comes to the stock market. We have to ask ourselves: do we believe that stocks will continue to do better than bonds, and bonds will continue to do better than cash, just as they always have?

If we can accept that basic framework, then temporary

declines, no matter how terrifying, are just part of the deal. While this doesn't make investing easy, it does make it easier.

Approaching investing based on the data from the past doesn't require you to ignore the tough economic challenges we face. It just requires that we believe we will find a way through them. I have no idea how we are going to deal with the massive public debt and everything else CNBC is throwing at us, but I do believe that we will get through it. Why? Because, to me, investing based on the weighty evidence of history seems the most prudent thing we can do. So far it has always proven to be correct. Every time someone has predicted the death of the stock market, they have been wrong. Given this record, isn't it reasonable to assume that stocks will continue to be better than bonds, and that bonds will continue to be better than cash?

If you agree, here are three principles based on scientific and historical data about how the market has performed over long periods of time.

1. Diversify your portfolio.
2. Keep your costs low.
3. There is a correlation between risk and reward.

1. Diversify your portfolio.

The first principle of investing is based on a simple concept most of us learned as kids: don't put all your eggs in one basket. While this may seem obvious to you, unfortunately, it isn't for everyone, so here's a basic overview of why diversification is so important.

□ ○ △ ✳

DIVERSIFICATION...

On the whole, the financial press isn't so keen on stories of people who've made sound investment decisions over four decades, paid down their debt, created a diversified portfolio, and reached their retirement goals on time or even a little ahead of schedule. Those stories don't sell magazines or have a very high click-through rate.

No, the stories we hear most frequently are those of the ultrarich whose investment strategies were not diversified, but rather concentrated in one stock—often the stock of a company they founded or worked at in its early days. Think of the Mark Zuckerbergs or Bill Gateses of the world. And while we applaud their successes with news and public celebration, what we forget is that betting on a single company often ends in failure.

We need a different strategy: diversification.

When we diversify our portfolios, we lessen the risk significantly of any one stock hurting us. We do so by eliminating "unsystematic risk" and taking on "systematic risk"—and here's how to tell the difference between the two.

When you hear people say, "I lost all my money in the stock market," it's because they've taken on too much "unsystematic risk." They thought Enron or Tyco was their golden ticket—and when those companies went under, they lost it all.

Unsystematic risks include:

A. *Betting on a particular industry or sector.* We see this in the form of trying to pick the next hot sector, such as technology, banking, or oil stocks.

B. *Owning individual stocks.* Owning individual stocks is the opposite of being diversified, because you have your hand in only one basket rather than in a number of them.

C. *Believing we can predict the market.* Whenever I say we can't time the market, people nod their heads. But as soon as some talking head weighs in with what seems to us to be detailed research about the direction of the market, we're quick to believe what they say.

What you want instead is to take on "systematic risk"—this means you're invested in the concept of capitalism as a whole. It's based on the assumption that, despite the up-and-down nature of the market (and how terrifying the "downs" are), over long periods of time, it will continue to grow. Therefore, you want to own hundreds of stocks across the market; sure, some of the companies you own will fail, but it won't really affect you because you spread your risk across a whole bunch. For instance, if you own ten thousand companies in the form of mutual funds, and ten or even twenty go bankrupt, you probably wouldn't even notice.

The magic of diversification is that you can take two individual investments, which when viewed in isolation are individually risky, and blend them in a portfolio. Doing so creates an investment that's actually less risky than the individual components and often comes with a greater return. In finance, this is as close as we get to a free lunch.

A well-diversified portfolio should include as many different kinds of companies as you can: U.S. as well as international companies, and a mix of small and large companies.

The easiest way to achieve that is through low-cost, diversified mutual funds. You'll end up owning different mutual funds that will spread your risk across every kind of company. To simplify this further, you could think of index funds as your default. Not only are they superdiversified, as mentioned above, they're also really low cost—and I'll explain why cost is important in a moment.

What Diversification Looks Like

Allow me to share the tale of four portfolios to demonstrate the power of diversification.

First, let's start with two undiversified portfolios:

- *Portfolio 1 is invested completely in the five hundred largest companies in the United States that make up the S&P 500 index.*

- *Portfolio 2 is completely invested in the international companies that make up the most popular international index, known as the MSCI EAFE index.*

Each portfolio is very concentrated: one in U.S. stocks, one in international stocks. So how has each of these portfolios done?

	Return	Risk
Portfolio 1	11.56	16.75
Portfolio 2	9.97	21.70

The table above compares two variables: the return and the risk of each portfolio. I've used the most common measure of risk: the standard deviation, which simply means how much something goes up and down. I'll spare you a painful return to statistics class. Just believe me: the lower the number, the better.

As you can see, the rate of return was similar, with Portfolio 1 returning 11.56 percent and Portfolio 2 returning 9.97 percent, and the standard deviation for Portfolio 1 was 16.75 percent and for Portfolio 2 was 21.70 percent.

Now let me show you the magic of diversification by blending the two portfolios.

- *Portfolio 3 is a simple mix of these two: 60 percent allocation to the same U.S. companies that make up Portfolio 1 and 40 percent of the same international stocks that make up Portfolio 2.*

How did it do?

	Return	**Risk**
Portfolio 3	11.21	16.81

Portfolio 3 had a return almost as high as Portfolio 1 but with far less risk than Portfolio 2.

What we just did was diversify between different kinds of stocks. While spreading your money among different types of stocks is valuable, the real power of diversification comes when we include safer assets like high-quality bonds and cash in your portfolio.

So let's introduce Portfolio 4:

- *This portfolio has the same stock allocation as the one we built in Portfolio 3, but to make it less risky, we're blending in a 40 percent allocation to bonds.*

So did we indeed reduce our risk?

Portfolio 4's return was 10.13 percent, a bit lower than the return we got from Portfolio 3, the all-stock portfolio, but not by much. But the real impact is in the risk reduction we see in the form of much lower volatility as measured by standard deviation at 10.52 percent.

That's a 37 percent reduction in risk!

The reason this matters is that having a less volatile portfolio over time means that you've narrowed the range of potential outcomes in the future.

While I'm not suggesting that this portfolio is right for every individual or serves as a predictive model, the point is: history shows us that diversification works.

2. Keep your costs low.

Lots of money has been spent—maybe more than on any sort of research, sadly—on trying to find "predictive variables" for the market. In other words: is there something about a particular stock, fund, or other investment—some defining characteristic—that can assure it will do well in the future?

Researchers have looked far and wide for these elusive variables: they've analyzed everything from whether funds are team-managed or solo-managed, where fund managers went to school and what kinds of research staff they have, to whether the president was a Republican or Democrat and which team won the Super Bowl that year.

And what did they find?

Sadly, not much.

It turns out that there's not a single variable that will help you identify how a mutual fund will perform—except for one.

Cost.

Which really just boils down to simple math: the more you pay for your investments, the less money you'll end up keeping.

3. There is a correlation between risk and reward.

No matter how hard investors try, we can't separate risk and reward. What that means to you is the more risk you take, the greater your potential return. This is as close to a universal law as we have in finance. Assuming that you're diversified and you've kept your costs down, the more risks you take, the higher return you can expect in the future.

HIGHER YIELD = HIGHER RISK

But before we go further, we need to define risk. We're not talking about risk with no payoff; what we're looking for as smart investors is *compensated risk*—the kind of risk that financial research has shown us leads to a greater reward. Here are some general rules of thumb for understanding compensated risk:

- *You're likely to get paid more for owning stocks than for owning bonds or sitting on cash. This is what's known as the "equity risk" or "equity return premium." Of course, it's riskier to own stocks than bonds or cash, but over longer periods of time—say, twenty-plus years—it's reasonable to expect a higher return. That's a perfect example of compensated risk.*
- *You're likely to get paid more for owning a basket of small companies than a basket of large companies. Why? Small companies are riskier, but if you take a chance on them, the payoff if they succeed is better.*
- *You'll get paid more for owning financially weak companies than financially strong companies. You may have heard of "value investments" and "growth investments." Basically "value investments" are financially weak companies: it's riskier to own them than "growth investments" (financially strong companies), but your potential reward is also greater.*

Why I Can't Just Tell You What to Do

Now that you're armed with a basic framework for a scientific investing strategy, here's where things get tricky. Because I know understanding the framework might be a good first step—but it isn't enough.

I know you want me to tell you what to do next.

I've been thinking about how to do that for more than a decade. In fact, the difficulty of this particular issue almost kept me from writing this book. I've been racking my brain, asking myself: How can I distill the hours I spend working with clients, linking their values and goals to a step-by-step plan, into some basic rules of thumb? How can I give you a one-size-fits-all set of guidelines when the whole premise of this book rests on the importance of creating your *own* financial plan?

After wrestling with this issue for months, I started sitting down with my colleagues from the BAM Alliance and asking them for their advice. One of the most illuminating moments came when I was having lunch with Jared Kizer, my firm's chief investment officer, who leads our investment policy committee. Jared's supersmart and really cares about the work we do because of the impact it has on people's lives. I waited until we were finished with lunch and waiting for the check before I brought up the topic.

"Hey," I said. "Let me ask you a question. Pretend I'm your best friend or brother and we're having lunch and you have five minutes before you need to get to your next meeting. And I pull out a pen and napkin and say: 'I've got this pool of money, how should I invest it?'"

"Well, first, I'd ask you what your goals are."

"We don't have time for that," I pressed him. "You have to tell me. I've got to go."

Jared asked me again for some details about my goals and values.

"We don't have time for that," I insisted, but I could feel the escalating sense of tension that came from his wanting to give the best answer. After all, we take this seriously. While we may say "money," what we're talking about here is people's most important goals. We went back and forth for a few more minutes and I finally said, "Sorry, Jared. You can't ask me any questions. You just have to tell me."

Finally, he gave up and said, "I *can't*."

Jared wasn't the only one of my colleagues struggling with this issue. Everyone I took through this little exercise pointed out to me that none of those one-size-fits-all answers you read about in all the investment books take into account people's unique needs. To do that, we all agreed, you need to meet with people, ask tons of questions, help them get really clear about what matters most to them. Only then could they come up with the "perfect portfolio."

And here's the dilemma that my colleagues and I suffer from. We want so badly to make sure that we give everyone the best advice we can that it's hard to give advice that's just simply "good." We lose sight of the fact that if we just gave you some "good" advice, we could help you build a portfolio that's most likely better than what you have now.

And so, as much as I want to assure you that the only perfect financial plan is one tailor-made for you, I do want to give you some guidelines for building a default portfolio and share some of the considerations you should keep in mind when tailoring it to suit your needs.

Building a Default Portfolio

Here's the issue with coming up with a perfect portfolio. I wish I could give everyone who bought this book twenty questions and use the answers to create a personalized spreadsheet—but the reality is that your plan is going to vary with what your goals are. It will involve a careful balancing act between how much you can reasonably save and your goals. It's as much an art as it is a science.

Since I can't walk you through this process, I'll instead share a "good enough" alternative that uses the institutional default of a 60/40 split between stocks and bonds.

There are, as I've mentioned, better ways than the 60/40 default. It reminds me of something John Bogle, founder of the Vanguard Group, once said when pressed to offer his own rule of thumb about how to build an investment plan: "There might be advice that's better than this, but the amount of advice that's worse is infinite." So, are there better ways? Sure. But will this default portfolio put you in a better position than a huge portion of the population? Yes.

1. Determine what you'll need in the next ten years. Leave it in CDs and savings.

2. Of the money you will not need for more than ten years, put 60 percent in the stock market with the following split:

   A. 18 percent of your total portfolio in international stocks. I often recommend the Vanguard Total International Stock Index Fund, though I have no affiliation with Vanguard.

    B.   42 percent of your total portfolio in U.S. stocks, such as the Vanguard Total Stock Market Index Fund.

3.   *Put the remaining 40 percent in safe, fixed-income bonds.* I recommend something low cost and diversified, such as Vanguard Total Bond Market Index Fund.

There's a reason 60/40 is the institutional default. Historically, it's worked.

But it's not without its problems.

- *It doesn't recognize the difference between your situation and anyone else's.*

- *It doesn't recognize your unique goals.*

- *It doesn't take into account your feelings about security and your ability to stick with a plan when the market is down.*

- *It doesn't take into account how much time you have.*

- *It doesn't factor in how much risk you can handle.*

Using Your Goals and Values to Customize Your Portfolio

While nothing can compare to a financial advisor walking you through this process of customization, I want to share some stories of clients who were able to use what they've learned from the values conversation to customize the default portfolio.

Scenario 1: A Dignified Retirement and Time to Travel

Greg and Brittany identified that security was really important, as was having enough money to provide for a dignified retirement and a lot of time with their kids.

First, we separated the list into short-term (within the next twenty years) and long-term goals (twenty-plus years out) in order to determine which money belonged in a savings account and which money should be split among stocks and bonds.

Greg and Brittany's long-term goals:

1. Dignified retirement (401[k])
2. Providing a solid foundation for their children
3. Some other long-term goals that were twenty years out, such as travel

Greg and Brittany's short-term goals:

1. Vacation fund (starting next year)

Here's how we determined their investment strategy and allocation:

1. We began with their short-term goals. It was pretty easy to see that they didn't want to put their vacation fund into the stock market because of all the risks we've talked about. Instead, they looked at the best-paying savings accounts at banks or online banks. They ended up buying a one-year CD, which they renew every year at a new rate.

2. Next, we looked at the 401(k) offered through Greg's employment. Because these plans often limit your choices, we went down the menu and found a broad-based U.S. stock market mutual fund with the lowest cost that was really diversified (it happened to be an index fund) and put 42 percent in that. Then we looked at international funds; they didn't have an index fund, so we found the diversified fund with the lowest cost and put 18 percent in there. We put the remaining 40 percent into a stable value fund that doesn't promise a lot of returns, but also won't move around a lot.

3. Finally, we looked at the money outside their 401(k)s for other long-term goals. Here, they felt like they could take a little more of a risk because the goals were so far away: they put 70 percent into the stock market (21 percent in international equities, 49 percent in U.S.), then put the remaining 30 percent into the lowest-cost superdiversified Vanguard bond fund they could find.

4. They made a commitment to stick with their plan, even when things get scary.

Scenario 2: Enough Time to Be Aggressive

My colleague Jordan recently asked me to help him as he and his wife were trying to figure out the allocation of her work 401(k).

Jordan and his wife are both young, have good incomes, and are in a good position financially. Because of their age and Jordan's knowledge of how the markets work, they were comfortable putting 90 percent in different types of stock mutual funds. While that may seem risky, they're young, Jordan's experienced, and they're committed to adding to it each month and ignoring the ups and downs of the market.

It's the "sticking with it" part that's so hard for many of us, but that can be more important than your actual allocation. Automate the allocation process, and don't think about it.

Scenario 3: Making Up for Lost Time

Since the last example dealt with a couple that had already begun saving money, let's switch gears a little. Say that you're in your forties and, for whatever reason, your financial plans got a little derailed. You poured all your savings into the kids' education, you made some bad investment decisions, you had to sell your house at a loss, you had to dip into your retirement account to get your business off the ground. You've been working hard for years, but only now are you in the position to really start saving. What do you do?

Given what has happened during the last ten years, there are many people in a situation like this. The last few years have been tough for many of us. If you find yourself in this position, you might want a 401(k) plan that's more aggressive than the 60/40 default—provided, of course, that you have the ability to take risks and stick with your plan.

Right now, my own 401(k) is 100 percent equity (diversified between U.S. and international stocks). I add to it every month and don't look at it at all. For now, I just accept that I'm still in heavy growth mode and will plan to add to it for the next fifteen years.

I hope these examples have been helpful, but I really want to drive this point home: this process is personal. These examples are merely here to show you how you might think about customizing your portfolio, based on your unique circumstances.

If you started with a 60/40 default and made some adjustments, you'd be a lot better off than if you did nothing. But ideally, you'll do as I did—spend some time talking this over with a financial advisor, a process I'll discuss in greater detail in the next section.

Rebalancing Is the Seventh Wonder of the Investing World

Your plan should include a commitment to stick with the split you choose between stocks, bonds, and cash. Of course, because the market is not stagnant, as time passes, your allocation will naturally shift. Periodically, you will need to go back into your portfolio and make sure the actual amount of money you have in each matches what it says in your plan. I recommend people rebalance once a year—and that they automate the process.

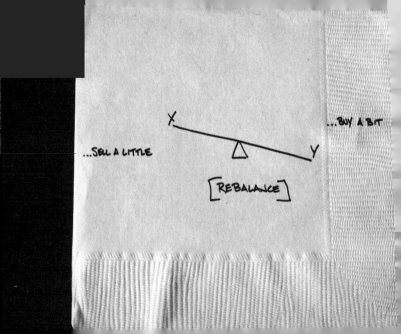

For those of you unfamiliar with rebalancing, this may seem like a hassle—but look at what's actually happening when you rebalance. Let's say you had $100,000 at the beginning of the year and you put $60,000 in stocks and $40,000 in bonds. In a year when the stock market did really well—say, increased by 30 percent—you'd have $78,000 in stocks. If the bond market stayed around the same, you'd now have $118,000, and instead of a 60/40 allocation, your allocation would be 66/34.

But, of course, that's not what you started with, so you're going to take that 6 percent and put it in bonds to bring your split back to 60/40. Doing this won't be easy, especially if the stock market is still doing well. But think about what you're doing: you're forcing yourself to take money from the thing that did well last year (sell high) and you're moving it to the area that did less well (buy low).

It's a totally unemotional way to buy low and sell high.

Let's say, on the other hand, stocks do poorly that year, leaving you with only 50 percent in stocks. You're going to have to grit your teeth and sell bonds to get yourself back to 60/40. It won't feel good to do it, but if you can accept what history has told us about markets—that they will always go up and down—this downturn will be temporary.

Prepare for a Crisis Before It Happens by Creating an Investment Policy Statement

A final thought about something important that I've yet to discuss: the time to prepare for a "market crisis" is long before you find yourself in one. No skydivers would try to figure out how a parachute works after they jump out of a plane; the same strategy is true for weathering the market's dips and falls.

We all know the stock market has its ups and downs. Yet, every time it plummets, too many of us go into a total panic.

The next time a market plunge has you ready to pull out of your investments, ask yourself: "Why so shocked? Haven't I learned this lesson by now?" We don't know when it will happen, and often it's hard to tell why, but the fact that the market went down should never surprise us.

To be clear: This is not a problem with the market. This is a problem with *us*. Any plan needs to account for the reality that markets go down as well as up. Part of the planning process must include a discussion about risk and even include lifeboat drills to see how you will react before you hit the water.

Remember what I said the research has told us about predictive variables? That, other than cost, they don't exist? Instead of getting hung up on predicting when the next downturn will occur, simply accept that it's inevitable, and focus instead on sticking to your plan when it does.

Since we seem to have such short memories, I suggest that once you've decided upon your allocations between stocks, bonds, and cash, you write down your rationale for your decision.

Keep your statement simple—it should be a couple of paragraphs long, one page at most. Lately, I've been suggesting that clients can also record themselves and keep the file on their phone. All that matters is that it reminds you of your goals and values and why you've chosen the plan you have—so I suggest doing this while the reasons behind your decisions are fresh in your mind. It can include your thoughts about how frequently you plan to revisit your 401(k) and rebalance.

This document or recording will serve as a touchstone to consult before you decide to do anything crazy. In the investment world, this document is called an "investment policy statement," or IPS. For our purposes, it's simply a contract with yourself to help you behave.

Use it to remind yourself that you picked your financial plan for a reason. Just because your 401(k) has lost value doesn't mean it's time to jump ship. Just because Jim Cramer is screaming at you to put your money in a completely different kind of instrument doesn't mean you need to listen. It's time to take a deep breath and do your best to ride out the storm. It's a way to remind yourself of that Stephen Covey quote I mentioned earlier: "It's easy to say 'no!' when there's a deeper 'yes!' burning inside."

PART FOUR

Strategies for Avoiding the Big Mistake

IF you follow what I've outlined in this book, you can create a financial plan that's aligned with your values and serves as a clear path forward toward your goals. However, if you don't stick to it, it won't take long for your plan to become another piece of scrap paper tucked away in a drawer.

The temptation to stray from your plan will, at times, be strong. As I've highlighted throughout this book, a lot of these decisions are emotional. No matter how hard you've worked to tailor your plan, you're still human. You'll still be tempted to make one of the two most common and costly "Big Mistakes" you can make as an investor: buying high or selling low.

Luckily, there are some ways that you can increase your chances of sticking to the plan you've created and avoiding either extreme. The first thing I'm going to suggest is that you get help. Why? Not because you're not smart enough to do it yourself—but because emotions will inevitably cloud your judgment.

Pretending that we aren't susceptible to emotion when it comes to these important decisions just increases the odds we'll head down the wrong path. Working with an objective third party can help you increase your chances of sticking to the right one. That person could be a friend, your father-in-law, a CPA, or an attorney. It could be a financial advisor, but you'll want to make sure you know how to find the right one, and that's what I'll be talking about in the next chapter.

The last bit of advice I want to share is also the most important:

Behave. For a really long time.

By now, you know what matters most to you. You can build the perfect budget. You can buy just the right amount of insurance. You could have the most efficient, beautifully designed portfolio in the world. But if you don't stick with it, it will all be wasted effort.

It's an incredibly simple idea, but it's one of the biggest hurdles to the process of making good financial decisions.

You'll need to behave over and over again. You'll have to do it in the face of unexpected circumstances. You'll have to do it when everyone around you seems to have lost their minds, and they're trying to tell you that "this time is different." And you'll have to do it even though it seems like you'll be missing the deal of a lifetime if you don't act now.

Of course, behaving is one of those things that's easier said than done. To arm you against inevitable temptations, I'm going to share some strategies for sticking to the plan you've created so that you don't undo all the hard foundational work you've done with one poor decision.

HIRE A "REAL FINANCIAL
ADVISOR"

A friend recently shared her decision to hire an expert after many years of managing her finances alone with her husband. Both she and her husband are incredibly smart, savvy, and successful. If you looked at their biographies, it would seem ridiculous that they needed help making sound investment decisions.

It took them a long time and a couple of different attempts to find someone who followed a process similar to the one I've outlined in this book. They went through the initial Discovery meeting, had some great conversations, and then decided to hire him. My friend is the first to acknowledge it wasn't an easy process, but it didn't take long for her to get a taste of how different her financial life would be working with an expert.

Based on some advice from their advisor, they were getting ready to make some changes to their investments because their old portfolio didn't match their goals at all. While she understood in principle that she'd need to make some changes, she was surprised to discover how emotional she felt about that.

I spoke to her right around the time she was going to sell her stocks and set up a more diversified portfolio, and asked her how things were going.

"Well, I know what we had didn't match my goals. I know it wasn't diversified and we need to sell. We're all on board," she said, "but I'm having such a hard time."

I asked her why.

"I own Apple!" she said, laughing. "And Lions Gate! They're really smart, they bought *Game of Thrones*."

"Look at them, they're so cute," she said, referring to the companies' logos. "I realize I'm literally treating my stocks like stuffed animals in my room. And now my advisor is going to take them out into the street and shoot them!

"It felt like my advisor was just dismissing my previous decisions," she said. "Then I stopped and realized how I talked about these stocks. I didn't own them because they were part of some bigger plan. . . . My reasons for owning them were about as legitimate as the reasons for keeping a stuffed animal.

"This is exactly why I need someone else involved. I'm getting way too emotional," she said, then admitted that she didn't simply own stocks that were thriving. "I also own JCPenney and BlackBerry."

———

I've tried to make the process of financial planning as simple as possible. However, you may still find that you want help in one or more areas, and that's okay. The important thing to remember is that if you want help, it's not because someone is smarter than you, but because *that person isn't you.*

As I've written throughout this book, a lot of these decisions are emotional. No matter how smart you are, you're still human. You'll still feel emotion around these incredibly important decisions, and to help you make the best decision possible, you'll find it helps to work with someone who isn't you.

The best explanation I heard for this approach came from a friend who also happens to be a very successful, and now retired, investment banker. I assumed that if anyone could figure it out on his own, it would be this guy. So when I asked him why he worked with an advisor, his answer surprised me.

"Carl," he said, "I could manage my own money except for the 'I' part." In other words, this successful financial professional was just as susceptible as his clients to making an emotional decision when it involved his money. By reaching out to an objective third party, be it an accountant, an attorney, or an advisor, you're asking someone you trust to shine a light on the blind spots that you, by definition, can't see.

In Daniel Kahneman's seminal book *Thinking, Fast and Slow*, the Nobel Prize–winning psychologist makes a very persuasive case for the premise that "it is easier to recognize other people's mistakes than our own." If you want more evidence that this is true, and you happen to be married, ask your spouse. I suspect he or she will know exactly what mistakes you've made and vice versa—even if you're each blind to your own errors.

I can't stress this point enough: You aren't looking to hire someone to make decisions for you. Instead, you're seeking experts who can provide a check and balance to your decisions. While some of you may feel perfectly comfortable making all of these decisions independently, others may have discovered through the discussions in this book that they'd prefer not to make some of these decisions alone.

The Secret Society of Real Financial Advisors

As important as I think it is to work with an advisor, I realize finding a good one is hard. That's because the traditional financial services industry is ill equipped to help us with the process I've outlined in this book. That said, as difficult as it is to find a great advisor, they do exist. I often joke that the ones you do want to work with belong to something I've dubbed "The Secret Society of Real Financial Advisors."

They're secret primarily because they're so busy doing the work that they don't have a lot of time left to promote themselves. But to help you find one of these elusive experts, I'll walk through what they usually look like (in other words, how they run their business), potential ways to find them, and the reasons why you want to work with them.

1. Real financial advisors diagnose before prescribing.

Imagine you went to the doctor, and the first words you heard weren't "How are you feeling today?" but "Everyone

I've seen today has the flu. I'm writing you a prescription for *X*"? That's it. No conversation about why you're at the doctor's, and no questions about your symptoms. You just get handed a prescription and the doctor disappears out the door before you have a chance to explain you're there for an allergy shot.

Way too often, the same thing happens when you meet with financial experts. You get a prescription after a cursory diagnosis that doesn't have anything to do with your situation.

This happened to me not too long ago. My wife and I made an appointment to meet with an estate attorney. Before we arrived, we were sent a questionnaire. When it came time for the actual meeting, it didn't take long for the attorney to propose two different solutions. Both were equally confusing. He was using language that didn't make any sense to us. The meeting came to a head when my wife had reached her boiling point. She said, "We didn't come here so that we could make this decision. We came here because we don't know what to do. Your job is to ask us a bunch of questions and get to know our situation well enough so that you can tell us what to do." Needless to say, we didn't go back.

So keep that in mind when you begin to meet with potential advisors. What should you be looking for? Perhaps this won't come as a shock, but I believe your first meeting should look a lot like the opening chapters of this book. Your advisor should be asking lots of questions to help him or her get to the bottom of what's important about money to you.

2. Real financial advisors are open about conflicts of interest.

We all understand the difference between an advisor and a salesperson. We would never expect a Toyota salesperson to send us to the Honda dealership if a Honda was better for our family. We know when we walk into the dealership that they are going to try to sell us a Toyota, and we're prepared to protect our own interests.

But things get confusing when salespeople call themselves advisors. I know of no other industry where it's harder to figure out who does what. Everyone in the traditional financial services industry calls themselves an advisor, so you would think that means they are giving you advice that will be in your best interest. And sometimes they are.

Other times, things aren't so clear. We have all heard plenty about advisors who clearly put themselves and the firm they work for ahead of the customers. There's a debate in the industry about how to solve this problem, but don't hold your breath. Instead, forget what they call themselves and who they work for and start asking yourself if your advisor or the one you're considering puts your interests ahead of their own.

If you have any doubts, have a very candid conversation. Ask them about conflicts of interest. Remember, this is not a foolproof way to find someone you can trust, but having these kinds of conversations will put you in a better place to carefully evaluate the nature of your relationship and act accordingly.

3. Real financial advisors are transparent about fees and compensation.

One really specific way to determine conflicts of interest is to follow the money. You need to understand how your advisor gets paid. Remember, it's all but impossible to completely eliminate conflicts of interest because money's being exchanged. However, you'll know you're on the right path to finding a real financial advisor if he or she is transparent and open to talking about those conflicts.

Here are two specific questions I suggest you ask: "How much do I pay you?" and "How are you compensated?" They might sound similar but they're two very different questions. That's because many financial advisors' compensation can include bonuses for meeting sales goals, spots on "educational" trips, or direct compensation for selling you certain products. So asking how they're compensated will help you identify any potential conflicts of interest.

An even more specific question you shouldn't be afraid to ask is, "Do you get paid (or win) anything based on the

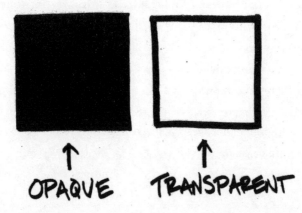

↑   ↑

OPAQUE   TRANSPARENT

products you recommend to me?" And try this one, too: "Do you receive compensation for our relationship from anybody other than me?"

Uncovering a potential conflict doesn't automatically mean it's something bad; it's just very important to know about it.

There are some financial professionals who are only compensated by you, the client. In other words, they don't get paid differently for selling different kinds of products. As Josh Brown noted in the *Wall Street Journal*, this model isn't perfect, but it does reflect an improvement in the financial industry:

> *There will always be conflicts, the world is not a perfect place, but we can say emphatically that the industry has come a long way. The major potential conflicts are washing away as the tide turns from brokerage to advisory but some small flaws still persist. And that's okay, so long as we're moving forward for everyone's benefit.*

As you ask these questions, you'll discover you'll feel most confident about the relationship when there's a clear, stated amount that you'll pay for a service. You may be billed monthly or quarterly, but you'll know exactly when you need to pay and how much.

4. Real financial advisors stand between you and the Big Mistake.

To a certain extent, the process of finding a real financial advisor is a qualitative experience. It boils down to the question

"Can I see this person getting to know me well enough so that I can trust him to help me behave for the next twenty years of my life?" Yes, you should verify that they're properly registered. Do a Google search of their regulatory record. I'm not talking about blind trust here—the kind that would allow someone to steal your money. I'm talking about finding someone who's willing to get to know your goals and values well enough to help you stick with your plan.

Remember, your financial advisor is the only one standing between you and the Big Mistake of buying high and selling low. You're hiring them to do what you can't: make unemotional decisions about your portfolio. If they can't do that, why pay them?

BEHAVE, FOR A REALLY
LONG TIME

A lot has changed since I began working in this industry almost twenty years ago, but one thing has remained constant: financial success is more about behavior than it is about skill.

In his brilliant book *Thinking, Fast and Slow*, Daniel Kahneman, the psychologist who won the Nobel Prize for pioneering the field of behavioral economics, noted that we all suffer, to some extent, from cognitive biases that make it nearly impossible to make good decisions. Our biases often cause us to take mental shortcuts that can thwart our efforts to successfully balance logic and emotion.

In an interview with Morgan Housel of *The Motley Fool*, Kahneman explained that while it might be possible for some of us to move beyond our biases, others are not so lucky. When Housel asked if these biases are genetic, the psychologist answered, "The biases that I've been concerned with are really characteristics, I think, of the way we're wired to interpret the world. So in that sense, yes, we're born with them."

In other words, unless you got really lucky in the DNA lottery, your biases will inevitably threaten your ability to make good financial decisions. Of course, you probably already know that. Even the smartest among us have done dumb things when it comes to our investments. Even if it seems irrational to you now, I promise you that the next time the market gets ugly, most people will sell. The next time it soars, most people will buy.

Does that mean we're doomed?

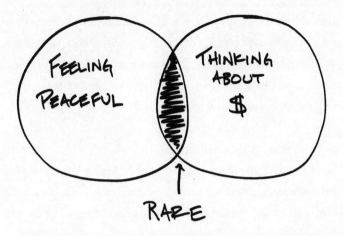

I don't think so. Yes, it's clear that cognitive biases are part of our genetic makeup. And, yes, it's clear that if we keep behaving as we always have, there's a good chance we'll end up with similar results. But what if we could do something to sabotage the part of our brain that is wired for bad behavior?

In fact, we can. There's an entire movement of life-hacking techniques built around the premise that we can set up systems and tricks that make it harder for our brain to derail good behavior. One of my favorite examples of a hack is my daughter's trick for remembering to put on her shoes before leaving the house. She leaves them right in front of the door, along with anything else she'll need for the day, so she literally can't open it without noticing the shoes.

The final step in creating your financial plan is setting up guardrails that make it very difficult for you to misbehave. You can think of these guardrails as metaphorical "shoes in front of the door" that will prevent you from running over the hot coals of the stock market unprepared. By putting some of these guardrails in place, you're establishing a kind of path for yourself—yes, it's a wide path with room to maneuver, but it will help ensure that you never stray too far from what's most important to you.

1. Have a plan—and stick to it.

By now, the reasons to create a financial plan should be painfully obvious. Building a strategy around your unique goals and values and recording the rationale behind your plan in an investment policy statement (IPS; see page 186 for a refresher) is perhaps the best way to avoid getting sidetracked. Why? Because you're going to be thrown all sorts of curveballs—fear when the market is scary, greed when it's doing well, temptation to splurge just this once.

Having a plan in place will serve as a touchstone when you're tempted to do something crazy. Your IPS will remind you about what you said was important when you weren't in the heat of the moment. Often, that simple act is enough to help you close your financial statements and get back to your gardening.

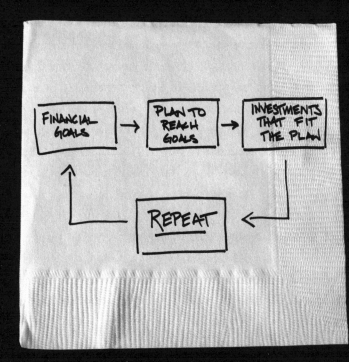

THE ONE-PAGE FINANCIAL PLAN

2. Automate good behavior.

I wrote a bit about automation earlier in the book, but it bears repeating because it's one of the best strategies for helping us stick to our plans. Instead of forcing yourself to make these decisions again and again, make them automatic so your good intentions can turn into good behavior.

You can automate your savings and your 401(k) allocations and make sure they're automatically rebalanced, and I also suggest automating certain set payments, like mortgages or car loans. In these situations, you've already accounted for these expenses in your budget. They're a set and known cost every month. You'll save yourself the time and effort if you make these commitments automatic.

The point is: by making these decisions automatic, the temptation to cheat will decrease.

3. Remember, remember, remember.

If there's one silver lining to our past financial mistakes, it's that we leave a trail. There are records of how you behaved in the past, both good and bad. Were you convinced that the Internet bubble of 1999 was never going to pop? Be honest; go look and see if you were buying Pets.com with your bonus money back then. Did you get scared out of the market in the decline of 2002? Did you try to get into real estate in 2007? And, of course, perhaps the most painful one: did you panic and sell in 2009? We can now look back and realize which of our decisions were mistakes. We might not be able to fix what we've done, but we can take note of patterns of behavior. We can remember how we felt and whether fear or greed caused us to make bad decisions. We might not be able to change how we feel the next time the market does something similar, but we can remember whether acting out of fear or greed has served us in the past.

4. Leave it alone.

Would you ever plant a tree and then go in every month and dig it up to see how the roots are doing? Well ... maybe some of the impatient among us might be tempted to, but all of us know we need to leave the tree alone for it to grow. The same is true of an investment plan. When done correctly, investing should look a lot like growing a giant oak tree. It's boring, but as Warren Buffett said, someone is sitting in the shade of an oak tree today because someone did the boring work of planting and taking care of it decades ago.

In other words, it might be "short-term boring," but in the long term, it's very exciting. What would happen if you tried to make the process of growing an oak tree more "exciting"?

Investing is one of those cool, rare things where we actually get rewarded for being lazy. Once you get it right, the less you do, the better. As Buffett said, "The hallmark of our investment process is benign neglect, bordering on sloth." How awesome is that? We've been looking for something like that our entire lives!

INVESTING DONE RIGHT

WATCHING GRASS GROW

BOTH ARE BORING !

Getting rewarded for doing nothing: Think of what that means! You can now channel your desire for excitement into time with your kids, trips with your spouse, and new hobbies.

What will you do with all that time you used to spend opening statements?

Whenever I tell people that I find financial planning exciting, this is what I'm talking about. I hope you're beginning to see the countless ways that creating your own financial plan pays off—and I hope I've convinced you that it's not just about the biggest retirement account and it's *never* about finding the perfect investment.

It's about giving you the time to do what matters most.

ACKNOWLEDGMENTS

Because this book represents the collective wisdom of all the real financial advisors I have worked with over the last twenty years, I would be remiss if I didn't acknowledge at least a few of them.

Specifically Matt Hall, Rick Hill, and the Hill Investment Group, Bill Morgan at Herbein Wealth Management, Jeffrey Cohen at Nova Wealth Management Group, the entire crew at Jackson Thornton Asset Management, John Garvey at Bland Garvey Wealth Advisors, and all the members of the BAM ALLIANCE. You serve as a daily reminder of what it means to be a real financial advisor.

The input from my colleagues at Buckingham and BAM was instrumental in shaping this book. Thanks to Adam Birenbaum, Al Sears, David Levin, Larry Swedroe, Tim Maurer, Jared Kizer, Dan Solin, Meredith Boggess, Aaron Vickar, and Manisha Thakor for your early reviews and ideas on how to make this book better.

I owe so much to Christy Fletcher, her team, and everyone that worked on this book at Portfolio.

Sarah Ramone was massively important in taking a pile of fifty thousand words of copy and helping me turn it into a book. She is a master of finding places to add and, more important, places to take away.

My team at Behavior Gap has been amazing. Special thanks to Britt Raybould for almost a decade of work and to Cara Jones for stepping in at the last minute to run my professional life.

Finally, I owe a huge debt of gratitude to my family, particularly to my wife, Cori, for her emotional support and insightful advice on everything! Of course the love and support of my kids, Ruby, Sam, Grace, and Lindsay, is what keeps me going!

NOTES

Introduction

1 http://www.nirsonline.org/index.php?option=com_content&task=
   view&id=768&Itemid=48.

Chapter 2: Guess Where You Want to Go

1 https://trends.collegeboard.org/college-pricing/figures-tables/
   tuition-and-fee-and-room-and-board-charges-over-time-1973
   -74-through-2013-14-selected-years.

Chapter 5: Save as Much as You Reasonably Can

1 http://www.nytimes.com/2012/02/25/business/another-theory
   -on-why-bad-habits-are-hard-to-break-shortcuts.html?pagewanted
   =all&_r=0.